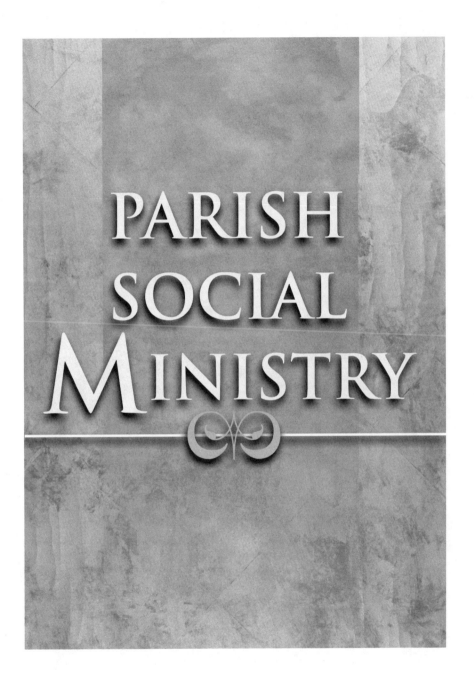

PARISH SOCIAL MINISTRY

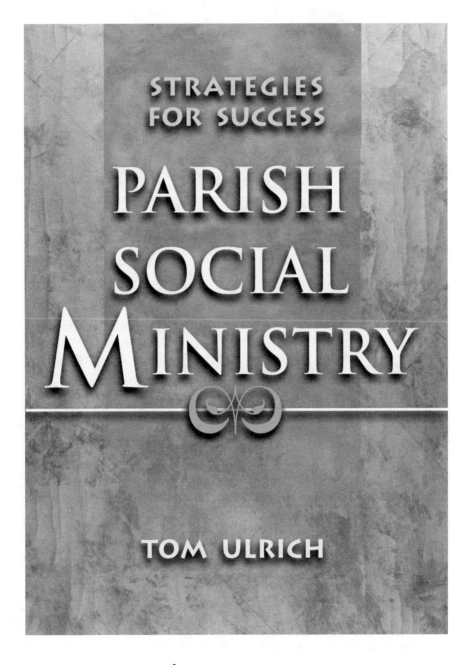

STRATEGIES
FOR SUCCESS

PARISH
SOCIAL
MINISTRY

TOM ULRICH

ave maria press   Notre Dame, Indiana

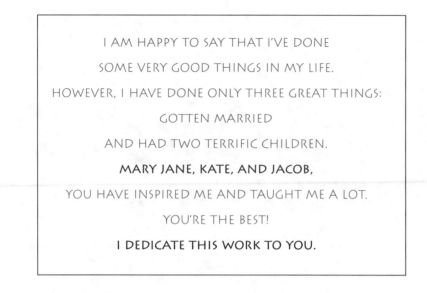

I AM HAPPY TO SAY THAT I'VE DONE

SOME VERY GOOD THINGS IN MY LIFE.

HOWEVER, I HAVE DONE ONLY THREE GREAT THINGS:

GOTTEN MARRIED

AND HAD TWO TERRIFIC CHILDREN.

MARY JANE, KATE, AND JACOB,

YOU HAVE INSPIRED ME AND TAUGHT ME A LOT.

YOU'RE THE BEST!

I DEDICATE THIS WORK TO YOU.

© 2001 by Ave Maria Press, Inc.

www.avemariapress.com

International Standard Book Number: 0-87793-747-8

Cover and text design by Katherine Robinson Coleman

Printed and bound in the United States of America.

Library of Congress Cataloging-in-Publication Data
Ulrich, Tom.
Parish social ministry : strategies for success / Tom Ulrich.
     p. cm.
     ISBN 0-87793-747-8 (pbk.)
1. Church work--Catholic Church. 2. Church and social problems--Catholic Church. I. Title.
     BX2347.2 .U57 2001
     261.8--dc21
                                           2001002529
                                                CIP

CONTENTS

Acknowledgments   6

Foreword by Fred Kammer, S.J.   7

PART ONE

Content Overview   9

Introduction   11

CHAPTER ONE   Vision and Mission   13

CHAPTER TWO   The Foundation of the Full Mission   18

CHAPTER THREE   Nine Key Elements of Success   25

CHAPTER FOUR   Organizing Leadership Teams   31

CHAPTER FIVE   Recruiting Leaders   35

CHAPTER SIX   Social Analysis   38

CHAPTER SEVEN   Integrating and Coordinating
                 the Parish Social Ministry Effort   43

CHAPTER EIGHT   Partners in Crime: The Diocese and the Parish   45

CHAPTER NINE   Being a Good Facilitator   48

CHAPTER TEN   Finally   49

PART TWO

Worksheets and Resources for
Effective Parish Social Ministry   51

ACKNOWLEDGMENTS

This modest contribution to the world of ministry has been an endeavor of love. Like any endeavor of love, it springs from the spirit and soul of many people (isn't community the heart of love?) and not just one person. With deep gratitude I acknowledge the following as friends, co-conspirators, co-authors, and just plain fun folks: Kristi Schulenberg, even though she is an extrovert; Dan Driscoll, editor extraordinaire; all the parish leaders with whom it has been an honor to work; and Mary Jane, the love of my life (for twenty-eight years and counting!). Thanks, gang! It's a real pleasure!

FRED KAMMER, S.J.

Past President, Catholic Charities USA, and author of
Doing Faithjustice: An Introduction to Catholic Social Thought.

Since the early 1970s, Catholic Charities USA has included a focus on parish social ministry that respects the baptismal commitment of every Catholic to serve Christ among people who are poor and vulnerable. Service to our members includes supporting the work of parishes in meeting the needs of their communities and linking Catholic Charities agencies to the Catholic in the pew.

Meeting the social needs of their communities—the elderly, teen moms, poor schools, blighted neighborhoods—is as essential to the life of the parish as the eucharist it celebrates. In fact, meeting the communities' social needs gives validity to the eucharist. It receives power from Christ who still today washes the feet of those he serves. The U.S. bishops wrote three key pastoral letters of the 1990s in which they urged such parish commitment: *Communities of Salt and Light* (1993) on the social mission of the parish; *Called to Global Solidarity* (1997) on parish responsibility for people at peril all over the globe; and *In All Things Charity* (1999) on the centrality of charity and justice to the life of faith.

No parish can serve all those in need within its boundaries. No agency can meet the needs of its community by itself. No church can heal the broken world alone. Parish social ministry is a vehicle to enhance the parish's desire to be Christ to the world. Parish social ministry helps the parish develop and support its own leadership in social ministry, create partnerships with Catholic social agencies and the wider church, and strengthen its linkages to other faith communities and the larger civic community.

Parish Social Ministry: Strategies for Success reflects this thirty-year history of service and support to parishes. Tom Ulrich of Catholic Charities USA performs an invaluable service in this book. His own extensive experience of working with parishes is an organizing spirit that weaves together the practical know-how of those at the church's grassroots, the informed expertise of a number of specialists, and the history of those who have spent the past thirty years laboring to make parish social ministry an integral part of Catholic Charities' contribution to low-income and vulnerable people.

This book also blends a rich stew of scripture, principles, social analysis, and key strategies with the practical know-how of organizing teams and even the more practical aspect of facilitating meetings. Anyone who has seen Tom in action knows that he combines in himself an effective knowledge of the scriptural, theological, and ministerial foundations of parish social ministry with extensive training, organizing, and facilitation skills. The book flows from the person, and the person enlivens the book's pages with both his firsthand knowledge and the lessons he has learned from women and men who make the church alive in communities across the country. Tom's patient listening and practical colleagueship have broadened his firsthand knowledge, thus making *Parish Social Ministry: Strategies for Success* a truly valuable resource. And he does it all with good sense and good humor!

This book is a good read, a handier-than-thou handbook, a primer for the neophyte, and a polisher for the skilled. It will be a useful companion for pastors, parish leaders, social agency personnel, and those longing to put flesh on the bones of their desire to connect faith to justice, sacrament to society, and Christ to the world we live in.

PART ONE

CONTENT OVERVIEW

This resource addresses the following topical questions. These questions are offered in order to give the reader a quick glance at the content covered.

QUESTIONS POSED AND ANSWERED IN THIS BOOK:

▸ What does a fully functioning parish social ministry effort look like? What is its vision?

▸ What does a parish social ministry effort attempt to accomplish? How does it attempt to accomplish it?

▸ What is the foundation of parish social ministry?

▸ What are the characteristics of direct service and social action ministry?

▸ What are the scriptural foundations for parish social ministry?

▸ What are the key elements of successful parish social ministry?

▸ How does one assess to what extent parish social ministry is being fully developed in the parish?

▸ What exactly is a parish social ministry leader? How do we identify potential leaders?

▸ How is a team of leaders organized to be the conduit for parish social ministry efforts?

▸ How do you effectively recruit parishioners to lead social ministry work?

▸ Is it important for social ministry to be integrated into the life of the parish? How is that accomplished?

▸ How can diocesan offices and parishes create a partnership to do parish social ministry?

▸ What are the main considerations and skills for being a successful meeting facilitator?

The reader will soon have answers to these questions and, hopefully, a pretty good picture of how to engage in successful parish social ministry. Have fun!

I've been at the business and ministry of working in parishes for quite some time now. That business has been to assist parishioners, people of good and holy will, to organize themselves in a way that allows them to more effectively respond, through their parish, to the problems confronting low-income and vulnerable people in their communities. We'll call this parish social ministry. I have learned far more than I have taught. It has been and continues to be a humbling but energizing experience. Therefore, I embark on this project to share a healthy portion of that learning in a manner that contributes to the growing body of knowledge influencing parish-based social ministry. In addition, the pressure is on because when I told my son of my intention, he was totally underwhelmed and simply said, "Dad, whatever you do, don't make it boring. And, don't tell any stories about your family, or, at least, me." I have already violated one of his conditions, and the one about being boring could take over at any time.

That confessed, the plan for this effort is to create a working document that is organized around the key components of successful social ministry based in a parish as defined and practiced by Catholic Charities USA, yet incorporates some universal concepts. Its foundation is collective experience, more an art than a science. I have great confidence that what is described really works because I have witnessed it.

We who do this type of parish work are in the world of ministry: in other words, doing, responding to, and acting on the gospel message is our bottom line. However, that doing, responding, and acting must be well thought out, planned, and disciplined because our time is too valuable to waste. My goal, then, is to present proven parish social ministry experience in a logical format that comes with the challenge to experiment with it. That experience is filtered through me but it incorporates a lot of excellent ideas, work, and practice from my colleagues in the field. (Four people in particular should be recognized: Kristi Schulenberg, Parish Social Ministry Director, Catholic Charities USA; Mary Wright, Education Coordinator, Catholic Campaign for Human Development; Bill O'Keefe, Director of Church Outreach, Catholic Relief Services; and Joan Rosenhauer, Special Projects Coordinator, Social Development and World Peace Office, United States Conference of Catholic Bishops.) The intention is to be clear, simple, practical, and direct. My hope is that it is helpful. I also hope it is not boring!

The book has been formulated with parish leaders in mind. Catholic Charities USA approaches the world of parish social ministry in a particular manner, which is my model for this book. However, the resource has a wider appeal. Anyone involved in leadership development for social ministry, including those in other faith traditions, could, with a bit of translating, cull critical organizing hints from these pages. I intend to provide some direction for leaders as they navigate their way through social ministry rapids, in whatever setting those rapids are found.

It is written in the sequence and with the content of a course or series of trainings on the topic of parish-based social ministry. It should be used to generate ideas and as a supplement to other resources, especially *Communities of Salt and Light: Parish Resource Manual* (Department of Social Development and World Peace, United States Catholic Conference). In addition, I have asked a few terrific folks who are up to their eyeballs attempting to do this work in their respective parishes (and succeeding at it!) to describe those efforts. Their words are interspersed in the body of the work in the hope that the reader will get some ideas and be inspired, as I have. Finally, books, even brilliantly written ones, can never take the place of training sessions. This is offered not to take the place of face-to-face training but to complement it.

CHAPTER ONE

VISION

AND MISSION

"**Y**ou can't build what you cannot imagine." Certainly, first imagining or having a vision of what one attempts to build applies to parish-based social ministry. During the final portion of a class in a social ministry course I recently taught, the participants were asked, "If you had a fully functioning social ministry effort in your parish, what would it look like?" The participants described a vision that was both revealing and, as far as I am concerned, right on the mark. According to the class's collective vision, social ministry would:

▸ Provide direct human service for individuals and families suffering the pain of poverty;

▸ Organize and join with those individuals and families to change the conditions that cause or exacerbate poverty, keeping in mind and acting on the fact that we are a part of the larger world in these matters;

▸ Initiate planned efforts to identify, train, and develop parish leaders, especially new ones;

▸ Create formation opportunities, ensuring that the social ministry work remains rooted in scripture and Catholic social teaching; and

▸ Establish a good communication system that keeps the entire parish and community connected.

The wisdom of the group captured the essence of parish social ministry. To that vision, however, please consider a few additional rudiments to fill out the picture.

The Catholic Charities Parish Social Ministry blueprint begins with baptism and the call each of us receives to actively participate in bringing about the reign of God. The United States Catholic bishops articulated this basic belief in their pastoral letter, *Economic Justice for All: Pastoral Letter on Catholic Social Teaching and the U.S. Economy*. The section titled "The Christian Vocation in the World Today" states:

> The Gospel confers on each Christian the vocation to love God and neighbor in ways that bear fruit in the life of society. That vocation consists above all in a change of heart; a conversion expressed in praise of God, and in concrete deeds of justice and service (Paragraph #327).

Further, the parish, as a constitutive part of its mission, provides an organized outlet for the community to respond to that baptismal call. The bishops developed this message in their document *Communities of Salt and Light*:

> We see the parish dimensions of social ministry not as an added burden, but as a part of what keeps a parish alive and makes it truly Catholic. Effective social ministry helps the parish not only do more, but be more—more of a reflection of the gospel, more of a worshipping and evangelizing people, more of a faithful community. It is an essential part of parish life (p. 1).

With baptism as the starting point, the mission of parish social ministry answers two connected questions: "What is parish social ministry attempting to accomplish?" and, "How is it trying to accomplish it?"

Simply stated, parish social ministry strives to assist parishioners, through the parish community, understand and act on Catholic social teaching. This is achieved by identifying, supporting, and training leaders who will organize people and activities around four specific, complementary ministries:

▸ Direct service such as emergency financial assistance, food baskets, home nursing, and job banks. Direct service provides a compassionate, yet empowering, response to the immediate pain of individuals and families in trouble. This is best done in partnership with organizations like the St. Vincent de Paul Society.

▸ Legislative advocacy networks where parishioners engage in efforts to create or change state and federal legislation to reflect just and compassionate social policy impacting people in poverty. This is best done in partnership with State Catholic Conferences and national Catholic organizations, such as Catholic Charities USA (Social Policy Division) and the Department of Social Development and World Peace of the United States Conference of Catholic Bishops.

▸ Global solidarity, including social justice and peace efforts, such as twinning with a sister parish in a different country, environmental stewardship projects, and world hunger or development programs. This is best done in partnership with Catholic Relief Services.

▶ Community organizing and community-based economic development projects that put into practice our passionately-held Christian belief in the rights and responsibilities of persons—especially powerless individuals, families, and communities—to fully participate in decisions that affect the quality of everyday life. This is done best in partnership with the Catholic Campaign for Human Development.

The common thread that weaves all this together is regular formation and reflection on Catholic social teaching. Such formation allows those involved to be confident that action arises from Catholic faith and values. Desire to build the City of God stays at the center of motivation for the enterprise, whatever the enterprise may be.

The chart below attempts to illustrate this parish social ministry mission in an integrated manner. The core is faith formation. Around that, much like an onion, are layers of the related but distinct ministries of direct service, justice and peace, global solidarity efforts, legislative advocacy, community organizing, and community development.

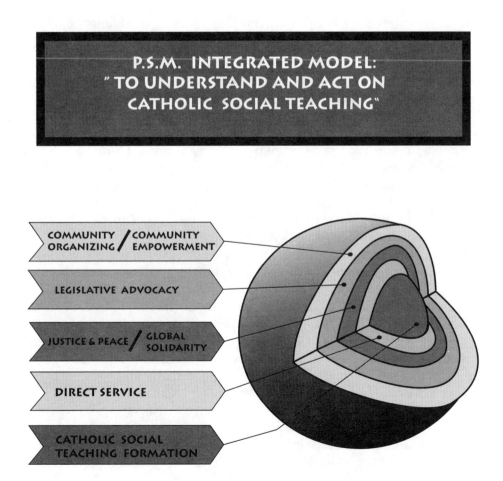

P.S.M. INTEGRATED MODEL:
" TO UNDERSTAND AND ACT ON
CATHOLIC SOCIAL TEACHING"

COMMUNITY / COMMUNITY
ORGANIZING / EMPOWERMENT

LEGISLATIVE ADVOCACY

JUSTICE & PEACE / GLOBAL SOLIDARITY

DIRECT SERVICE

CATHOLIC SOCIAL
TEACHING FORMATION

While each of us is called to be engaged in social ministry and the parish has a responsibility to create organized opportunities for that to happen, experience has told us that if parish social ministry is to become a reality, parishes need some assistance. Since I have been engaged with parishes in this effort, I have found that they, most often, request help in five critical areas:

▸ Planning the work and training leaders.

▸ Locating concrete action vehicles that will serve as a way to integrate parish efforts, not simply create new efforts alone. (Translation: "Parishes are very busy places. Do not try to make us do anything that is outside our parish mission! The best assistance is to provide opportunities for building community, not roadblocks! Help us be creative but connect us to models and people that work!")

▸ Finding supplementary written, audio, and video resources that support social ministry development in the parish.

▸ Offering formation and educational processes that keep those involved connected to the radical example of Jesus.

▸ Coming together (networking) with like-minded parishioners in order to support each other and discover new ministry ideas.

A side, but crucial point: While it is true that each baptized person is called to know and support this full vision of parish social ministry, it is also true that time, interest, and talent limit each person's ability to fully participate in all the ministry necessary to make a difference. How then can this apparent contradiction be reconciled? First, I strongly suggest that it would not be wise for anyone to even attempt to be involved in everything. (Although there are some who try, and you know who you are!) It cannot be done, so stop feeling guilty! On an individual level, pick something you have a passion for and do it. After some time, leave that ministry and move on to something else to widen and freshen your experience. (But do not forget to get someone to replace you on the ministry team you are leaving.)

I offer this example from my own life. For several years I was on the leadership team for my parish's involvement in a congregation-based community organization. After some time, I decided to move on. Other leaders needed to surface, and I had pretty much given what I could, from a leadership perspective. Although I continue to strategically support the community organizing work of my parish when I can by attending rallies and house meetings, I am not particularly involved. Instead, I am now a member of my parish's St. Vincent de Paul Society. I spend more time engaged in direct services like doing home visits and distributing Thanksgiving baskets.

Each person's contribution should be directed toward the full mission, but an individual cannot and should not take on the full mission itself. One must understand and support it but not attempt to do everything. What is imperative is that the PARISH is involved in the full mission of parish social ministry and offers opportunities in it. If a parish does less, it fails in its responsibility as a parish. A community can do it, an individual cannot.

In summary, the full mission of parish social ministry is to help parishioners understand and act on Catholic social teaching. It does that by organizing teams of leaders in (at least) the four ministry areas of direct service, legislative advocacy, global solidarity and global justice and peace, and community organizing. Those leaders, in turn, invite and recruit the rest of the parish to participate. Finally, all the activity is reinforced through formation and education in Catholic social teaching.

CHAPTER TWO

THE FOUNDATION

OF THE FULL MISSION

Before moving forward, it may prove instructive to spend a little time and reflective energy in digging deeper into the mission as described. By doing so, the foundational premise of parish social ministry will emerge. That foundation will be in Jesus' teaching and his example.

The United States Catholic bishops state that our vocation as followers of Christ is to praise God through concrete deeds of justice and service. What exactly are they talking about? What are deeds of service and justice? In fact, that question has already been answered. Such deeds include both direct service and social action (or action on behalf of justice). However, for clarity's sake, what are the characteristics of direct service and social action?

While I do not believe they are disconnected actions, they are distinct. Direct service has, at least, these characteristics:

▸ The focus of action (ministry) is to alleviate immediate pain, need, or crises. (For example, a family is in need of housing because of an eviction notice, and the minister helps them secure enough money to pay the rent.)

▸ The duration of the action is relatively short (as much time as it takes to pull together the funds for the rent).

▸ The solution deals with the effects of a problem, not the causes. (A family is being evicted. Get the money or they will be homeless. The fact that the community has little affordable housing [the primary cause of the problem] is important but not until that rent is paid and the family is safe).

▸ While there may be many people in need of direct service (in our example, many families facing eviction notices because they cannot afford the rent), ministry occurs on a one-to-one basis—one family at a time.

▸ The ministry relationship is one of "giver" of resources and "receiver" of resources. (In the best and most grace-filled direct service situation, this is

18

a compassionate, caring, nonjudgmental relationship. However, someone is always the giver and the other is the receiver. That is simply the nature of the ministry.)

▸ In our culture, direct service in not controversial. It is generally (but not always) expected and seen as admirable.

The characteristics of social action, as compared to direct service, consist of the following:

▸ The ministry focus is on the social problem, not the crises of an individual person or family. (In our example, the problem would be affordable housing as a community issue, not the specific family who is facing eviction.)

▸ The action takes a long time to unfold. There is research, planning, and mobilizing of persons to accomplish, which takes time. And, when a solution occurs, it will be of lasting duration.

▸ The solution is directed toward the cause of the problem, usually a law, institutionalized policy, or social practices that need changing. With the housing example, the solution may lie in changing a zoning ordinance (law) or a lending practice (policy), or addressing racial discrimination (social practice).

▸ The service provided is leadership development such that those leaders learn how to do the research, create strategies, and build a base of followers.

▸ Those community leaders can then mobilize large numbers of people and their resources to generate the power necessary to change laws, institutional policies, or social practices.

▸ The ministry relationship is one of equals working together in an organized way toward a common goal. The relationship dynamic is one of a partnership, including folks who are poor in the decision-making process.

▸ Such organizing for change is often quite controversial.

It should be noted, with great emphasis, that these two approaches to ministry (and their many variations) are each necessary and equally important. Both have a critical place in the world of parish social ministry as defined in the stated vision. In fact, some would argue (and I would be one of them) that direct service and social action are inextricably woven together.

With this clarification of what the bishops are referring to in their definition of the Christian vocation to praise God through deeds of justice and service, the next step is to find similar evidence in the gospel. By taking some time to thoroughly examine Luke 10:25–37 (the story of the Good Samaritan), I believe one will be able to clearly locate support for this line of reasoning. Try the following scripture reading exercise with a parish social concerns team.

DIRECT SERVICE & SOCIAL ACTION EXERCISE

THE GOOD SAMARITAN

LUKE 10:25-37

Read the above passage and ask the team which type of ministry is being highlighted. Chances are very good that the participants will, correctly, focus on Jesus' command to care for our wounded sisters and brothers, so direct service would be the answer.

Now, remind the participants of what was going on, historically, at the time this story was being told. That would include such factors as:

▸ Israel was an occupied territory of the Roman Empire.

▸ Jews were an oppressed people.

▸ Most Jewish religious leaders and wealthy families (as opposed to common folks) were viewed as the real chosen people because of their status.

▸ Most Jews were poor.

▸ Samaritans were hated. They were viewed as traitorous scum.

Re-read the scripture passage, keeping the historical factors in mind.

After the reading, state that the real drama of this scripture passage is the confrontation between Jesus and the lawyer who was trying to trap Jesus. In addition, the hero role model is a despised Samaritan whom Jesus lifts up as one to be admired and imitated. Jesus forces the learned and honored Jewish leader to admit that the hated Samaritan is neighbor.

Ask what type of ministry this story is calling for. The answer should now be social action in that Jesus is clearly demanding that to be one of his followers, we must change social practices (in this case, the attitudes toward and discrimination against Samaritans) to reflect the love of God.

Finally, explain that this passage is clearly challenging us to engage in the compassionate action of healing (direct service) AND in changing deep, institutionalized social attitudes (social action). Both ministry forms are necessary in order to truly live out the command to love!

I hope that the foundation of parish social ministry is made evident through this examination. Social ministry stands solidly on and in Catholic social teaching and holy scripture. For me, this constant reminder of our root provides the confidence and inspiration for continuing to plow ahead in what can sometimes be very difficult work. It actually makes me smile and even a little smug, in a holy sort of way, of course!

GREAT PARISHES, GREAT IDEAS

Our best resource is each other. We learn from others' best practices. Take a look at the way this parish combines direct service with social action. See how the openness of the Parish Social Ministry Director to the "messiness" of this ministry bore much fruit.

ST. EDWARD CONFESSOR PARISH

Diocese of Rockville Centre, New York

Rev. Joseph McComiskey, Pastor

Ms. Dawn Ravella, Parish Social Ministry Director

(reflection written by Dawn Ravella)

When I began my position as Director of Parish Social Ministry, there were seven programs in place. The office, then titled Human Services, had existed for eleven years, and was an excellent operation. Today there are as many as fifty-seven programs. There was never a grand scheme in my head to create all of these programs. It unfolded this way as people came forward with ideas and suggestions. There are about 150 volunteers. From the beginning, I knew that I should not begin a program if it depended on my running it. So all suggestions were welcomed, but there needed to be a volunteer to agree to be in charge before I would continue. This philosophy enabled such growth in the programs and participation. I had to face the fact that this kind of growth did not always allow for a smoothly run, efficient operation. I could not be in control to run all of the details the way I might have chosen. But the programs did not belong to me. They belonged to the people who were running them.

Parish social ministry is about building community. The premise is to call forth every member of the community to use their God-given gifts and experiences to minister to one another. Each of us has strengths and weaknesses, but when we pool our gifts, we fit together like a puzzle; one person's gap or weakness is filled in with another's strength. This philosophy would conclude that we need the contribution of each of our members, otherwise the puzzle would never be completed.

Parish social ministry can begin with meeting the obvious basic needs of community members. People come to the church and request assistance for basic needs like food, shelter, and clothing. Systems are put into place to respond to these needs, such as a food pantry and distribution of other in-kind resources. We serve approximately 115 families a year. There are currently forty-seven families that receive ongoing assistance year-round, while the remainders are families that just need a little extra help around the holidays. Drives are planned throughout the year when we are aware of extra expenses; for example, back-to-school drives for new sneakers, school supplies, and new clothing.

In my experience, people are very generous in the sharing of their own food and clothing. It makes people feel very good about themselves to share their resources, especially with someone from their own neighborhood. However, our obligation is so much greater than just meeting a person's basic needs.

In explaining parish social ministry, I like to quote Mother Teresa who said that a person in need is Jesus in disguise. If it really were Jesus who was asking for help, we certainly would not just hand him a bag of food. We would do everything within our power to help him be a fully functioning member of the community because we know how important his contribution is. I would like to suggest that each person coming for assistance be treated this way. We need to recognize and know how deeply special and sacred their gifts and potential are.

While we need to offer immediate help, we also need to ask the question "Why does this problem exist? Why does this person need food (or rent money, help paying the electric bill, or whatever)?" We need to take a good look at the entire big picture. We always want to address the "why" so that a person can get out of such a humiliating circumstance.

Many times there is a family crisis like a job loss, a divorce, a death, or an illness in the family. This is often temporary, though a very painful time. We call members of the community who have had similar experiences to walk the journey with this person in crisis, with understanding and compassion. This is where many support groups are formed. Someone whose spouse has died and has gone through the grief process may then be trained to help support others through this process.

A man who was out of work came to the parish for help. We were supportive through this process until he was back in action. Now he runs our entire employment program. We are always keeping our eyes open for successful job seekers who may want to come back to volunteer.

It is beautiful to see how people will reach out to one another after having shared a painful experience. This sharing is very powerful and very healing. I witness this all the time. I facilitate the process by watching closely for appropriate leadership—people who may need to be personally invited. I provide training and support, I offer meeting space on site at the church, and I link appropriate people together. Many groups are organized in this way, such as a divorced and separated group, a child bereavement group, a caregivers group, etc. For me, watching these groups form and journey together through painful places has been a true experience of the gospel in action. What is exposed time and time again is a side of humanity not often publicized in the paper or the focus of media attention: the genuine goodness of people and the willingness to help when confronted with a painful situation.

The church is the centrally located place that facilitates and organizes the community to be able to respond to one another. A pool of attorneys organized so that when a person is in need of legal counsel, we can go to them. It works this way across the board—therapists, doctors, family mediators, and financial planners are organized. These volunteers from the community are called upon when other community resources are not available. They assist the people who are falling through the cracks, so to speak. So, for example, if a person can afford to pay the attorney or is eligible for legal aid, then I would certainly not request a volunteer attorney to do it pro bono.

Sometimes when a person or family comes for assistance, it is an ongoing chronic difficulty and needs to be addressed in a different way. Sometimes we need to address the very structures of our community or society at large. For instance, a person who works full time making minimum wage in New York most often cannot make ends meet because of a shortage of affordable housing. This needs to be addressed on a much broader level than within the individual family. We need to address the access (or lack thereof) to skills-training and educational opportunities in order to help people move beyond minimum wage.

We try to organize and meet regularly with the heads of different houses of worship and leaders from those communities to work together on community issues. The power of this became quite evident at a recent public hearing when the heads of many houses of worship in the area were present to show support for the building of a controversial senior housing development.

Our pastor meets regularly with the heads of local houses of worship. Their relationship is a witness to the community. An unfortunate fire recently destroyed the worship space at St. Edward, and the other congregations were immediately offering support. We were invited to use the Lutheran church for daily Mass.

I meet regularly with representatives of each congregation whose work is comparable to mine. These relationships have proven beneficial on many levels. We have assisted each other by helping with families in the area, collecting food for the pantry and other drives, and we have received a great education about the commonalities of people of faith, whatever the particular denomination.

Our pastor is also a board member of the diocesan Catholic Campaign for Human Development (CCHD). He is part of a committee that reviews applications and makes decisions regarding funding groups that address the needs of the community. Education at the parish level consists of distribution of literature as well as representatives from CCHD-funded groups speaking to the congregation at Masses. The Journey to Justice process was a very powerful experience for those who participated (see p. 104). There was a ripple effect to the larger community. A group of people who continued to meet after Journey to Justice ended decided that social change would begin with small faith communities. After researching many existing groups, they decided to begin with RENEW, which has now taken a large portion of the congregation through many seasons. Many involved in this process are now getting ready to move forward and seek possibilities to work for justice.

We also lobby and dialogue with politicians regularly on broader issues. This year some of the things we spoke about were affordable housing, welfare reform, school vouchers, and partial birth abortion.

We have a committee of people dedicated to working on political issues through the lens of Catholic social teaching. This committee is called the Public Policy Education Network (PPEN).

The United States Catholic Conference published a statement on political responsibility called *Faithful Citizenship*. The message of the document was the same message our PPEN committee has been declaring since its inception; that as Catholics, we are obligated to educate ourselves on political issues in light of scripture and Catholic social teaching. The document says that we need to dialogue with politicians on these issues, examine our consciences, and vote accordingly on the full range of issues in light of church teaching. This PPEN committee speaks at the Masses using gospel reflections to show how these issues need to be addressed. We have voter registration drives and forums to educate the people through an open discussion of the pressing issues.

There are also global issues to confront. As Catholics we believe that we are all brothers and sisters in Christ, so global issues such as world hunger, debt in third world countries, landmines, etc., are on the agendas of our peace and justice committees. We try to educate ourselves, raise awareness in others, and dialogue with politicians on these issues when appropriate. Sometimes these issues are made more real when we show how we can make an impact. A good example of a success is "Sweat Free NY" that organized many of the schools not to purchase uniforms or equipment from any company that uses sweatshops or child labor.

Witnessing this work leaves my heart bursting with optimism for the future and a true appreciation for the church. I am so proud, fortunate, and grateful to be a part of it.

CHAPTER THREE

NINE KEY ELEMENTS

OF SUCCESS

Having established the parish social ministry mission and framework for guiding that mission, now what? What must be done to successfully develop social ministry in your parish? What are the key elements that must be attended to if your parish is going to be successful at starting and maintaining a social ministry effort?

Over the past several years, numerous conversations have been held with both diocesan and parish leaders doing successful parish social ministry. One purpose of these discussions was to specifically address the above questions. The process is not especially scientific. It has, however, produced a body of experience that has proven instructive. An analysis of that experience points to at least nine elements of successful parish social ministry. There may be more, but I am very confident that if significant portions of these elements are present, successful ministry will occur. Our collective findings suggest that parish social ministry will be successful if the following are true:

▸ *The parish social ministry effort is linked to faith development.* If Jane and John Parishioner are to participate in the ministry, they must feel that their work is not only doing good deeds, but that it also reinforces and strengthens their faith life.

▸ *It is evident and clear that what is being done is bringing about a more just, loving world.* The parishioners need to feel that they are contributing to a better world if they are to stick with the social ministry effort. They must believe that their small part is somehow helping to bring about God's reign.

▸ *The effort touches a system of values.* The parishioners must be able to see that the effort is right and just. They must have a sense of passion about the work.

▶ *Parish social ministry provides leaders with an opportunity to explore the deeper social, political, and institutional causes of problems and issues being addressed.* Parishioners must be given time, in a structured way, to explore *why* the problems being addressed exist in their communities and world. In other words, they must be able to engage in some social analysis. (This is most effectively done in collaboration with those experiencing the problems most directly.)

▶ *It is focused, and it addresses the full mission of social ministry.* Parishioners operate best when the activity is well planned and when opportunities to engage in direct service, legislative advocacy, global justice and peace efforts, global solidarity efforts, and community organizing—the full mission—are present. They know they will have various chances to select what they can do and what they want to do, broaden their experience, utilize their talent, and not waste their valuable time.

▶ *There is a focus on recruiting leaders in an ongoing and systematic way.* The plan must have a clear, uncompromising strategy THAT IS FOLLOWED to locate and invite parishioners to create and participate in the social ministry effort. Otherwise, the full mission cannot be addressed. It is that simple. THIS IS CRITICAL!

▶ *Thought and planning goes into organizing and developing leadership teams.* Parishioners are taught the basic steps for bringing a team of leaders together and are provided skills-building opportunities to make the work more efficient and rewarding.

▶ *The parish social ministry efforts are known, integrated into, and supported by the entire parish community.* The parish is aware of and embraces the ministry effort. There is a communication system in place that fully informs the pastoral team (priests, pastoral ministry staff, and the parish pastoral council) about social ministry activities. In fact, the system is so strong that the actions are truly taken in the name of the pastoral team and parish. Social ministry is never viewed by parishioners as something that a few "crazies" are doing. Instead, it is seen as an integral part of parish life that constantly welcomes and actively invites all parishioners to participation. Eucharistic liturgies incorporate social ministry in the celebration. The parish school and adult education efforts include the theology and practice of social ministry as part of the curriculum.

▶ *The parish and the parish social ministry team involve the people experiencing the problems in attempting to solve them or ease them.* The one who can best speak to both the impact of and solutions for the problems is the one experiencing the problems addressed in the parish social ministry efforts. That person has to be invited to participate. It makes sense from a practical and theological point of view.

Assuming these reflections to be true, what now to do with them? I have always felt that the best place to begin social ministry is by being clear about what exists. In that spirit, the "Nine Elements of Success" have been incorporated into an assessment tool. Its purpose is to provide a systematic way to compare what the parish currently has in place relative to the nine elements and to identify both strengths and weaknesses.

Of course, there is an element that I don't explicitly include among the nine, but I believe it to be critical. We'll call it the yarn element, because it is knitted into the very fabric of a successful parish social ministry effort, and in many ways it holds it all together. If you pull too hard on this yarn and try to remove it, you run the danger of unraveling all the elements. Our yarn element is *celebration*.

Celebrate every small success. Celebrate each other. Plan time together outside the parameters of the project or the action. Have fun. Remember that the Christian life is joyful. When "social justice types" are seen enjoying their work and each other, they are irresistible. People want to be around happy people. The problems we encounter are draining, so we must dedicate ourselves to celebration or we will wear ourselves out. I cannot emphasize this enough. Celebrate. Don't let it all unravel.

ASSESSMENT AND PLANNING EXERCISE

Gather a small group of leaders (three to ten people). They can be an existing social concerns committee, the pastoral team, or a group you have assembled specifically for this exercise. Follow these steps:

▸ Copy and distribute to each member the "Parish Social Ministry Success Worksheet" that can be found on page 53.

▸ Complete the worksheet individually and without comment. (Take approximately fifteen minutes for this, or until everyone is finished.) Instruct everyone to be completely honest since that is the only way the exercise will be helpful.

▸ Facilitate a process to discuss the results. Give everyone a chance to share. Spend time talking about why you see your organized (or disorganized, if that happens to be the case) parish social ministry world this way. However, try to identify the common thinking. Spend about forty-five minutes (or more if needed) on this.

▸ Attempt to move the group toward agreement on three things:

   ▸ your effort's primary strengths,

   ▸ the primary areas needing attention, and

   ▸ three to five specific tasks—emerging directly from this assessment—which your committee, group, or team will address in the next year.

The completed assessment sets the course for the coming year. This exercise can also be used on various other occasions, depending on the desire to determine where the ministry effort is at any particular moment. I recommend, however, that your group perform an assessment at least annually. The theory is that by following this assessment and planning formula, the parish's social ministry capacity will be built, over time, in specific areas toward an articulated, definite vision.

After reading about another great parish, let us turn our attention to how to build that capacity in three of the most crucial elements: organizing leadership teams, identifying and recruiting leaders, and the skill of social analysis.

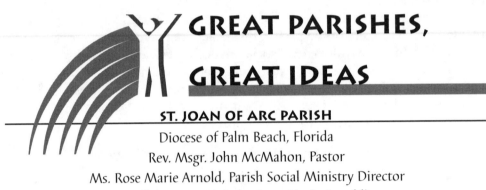

GREAT PARISHES, GREAT IDEAS

ST. JOAN OF ARC PARISH
Diocese of Palm Beach, Florida
Rev. Msgr. John McMahon, Pastor
Ms. Rose Marie Arnold, Parish Social Ministry Director
(reflections written by Rose Marie Arnold)

St. Joan of Arc Church is fortunate to have a very active legislative action ministry. Its mission statement expresses the desire to be informed, so biweekly meetings focus on issues that impact our Catholic moral and social justice values. The social action ministry invites the parish community to participate in legislative action through periodic seminars, panel discussions, and open community forums.

This ministry traces its roots to parishioners who took part in the Catholic Campaign for Human Development Journey to Justice Process and the Respect Life Ministries. Several years ago, members from these two groups went to Tallahassee for the Florida Catholic Conference and became inspired and concerned about health care. This was during the time that national health care bills were being debated. They came back and organized a seminar on the health care issue, and opened it to the community at large. This was an opportunity to express "Catholic thoughts" to the general public.

The group continued to meet and formed a mission statement to start a legislative action ministry. They began to attract people who were interested in advocacy. The group has five to six active members. Through the diocesan Respect Life Office and the Florida Catholic Conference they establish the necessary links to inform themselves of bills before Committee, and the contact information for legislators to whom they can respond regarding the issues. They send representatives to Tallahassee to visit legislators and present arguments for and against pending bills. Speakers from the community, the Florida Catholic Conference, other faiths, and legislators are invited to participate in seminars, making sure the position offered by the Florida Catholic Conference is well presented.

The legislative action ministry follows guidelines when having debates and forums. First they make sure those presenting the Catholic position are good, strong speakers. In addition, they always investigate the speakers and their knowledge of the topic. They collect speakers' biographies and give them a written format of the program. Literature on the issues is available as handouts. Generally, the speakers make their presentations and the audience is invited to write questions to be addressed later. During a fifteen-minute break, questions are evaluated and several picked for the speakers to answer. About thirty minutes are allowed for the questions. Sometimes legislators admit to learning from the audience what the real concerns are that they hadn't considered.

The legislative action ministry has been successful, but the work of inviting others to join them is sometimes difficult. Its members found some pastors reluctant to address political issues. Also, other congregations didn't seem to have a group consensus on the issues and were not organized. The legislative action ministry made presentations to women's and men's ministries and respect life groups in the area, and they found it difficult generating enough interest in the issues. In order to be successful and be true advocates, people must remove their (sometimes-partisan) political hats and put on Christ to change the world.

The legislative action ministry's goals for the future are to continue making an interfaith effort and focus on faith communities who share same views. This may help Catholics take a closer look at issues. Our voices DO make a difference, as we bear witness to the continuing mission of Christ through his church.

St. Joan of Arc Church is excited to have branched out into community organizing. Developing Interfaith Social Change (DISC) was organized as an interracial, interdenominational ministry that had its roots in the Catholic Campaign for Human Development and the Journey to Justice process.

An initial group of eight people began monthly dialogue sessions with a small group of Baptists. We met in the Baptist church, enjoying prayer, bible study, lively discussion, and warm fellowship. In 1994 the group was instrumental in having Martin Luther King Jr. Day finally recognized and properly celebrated in the city of Boca Raton.

In 1995, we formally organized as DISC and moved our location to a community room in a nearby public housing development. Our numbers increased to about twenty and we defined our mission. We were grounded in a desire to serve those struggling with poverty, and we continued to acknowledge the presence and power of God. In addition, we wanted to work in ways that

- motivated people of diverse backgrounds to join together,
- strengthened and supported natural leaders,
- promoted more justice in community affairs, and
- helped people share what they had with others in need.

Over the last five years, DISC members have become actively involved in the needs and concerns of Pearl City residents. Pearl City is located in the heart of Boca Raton and is home to many low-income people. We've organized community picnics and held a prayer breakfast for Baptist, Catholic, and Methodist pastors to enjoy fellowship and to reflect on how they might better help their people. We've joined parents in addressing serious problems in their area, and have organized conferences of parents, city and state legislators, and the press.

DISC members contribute service time and some funds to Boca Helping Hands, an interdenominational lunch program and food pantry held in Pearl City at Friendship Baptist Church. We also played a leadership role in establishing a memorial park to honor Dr. Martin Luther King, Jr. that has served to bring new respect and interest to the Pearl City neighborhood. Most recently we were asked to coordinate an intensive parish program based on the JustFaith model. This program explores the social justice teachings of the Catholic church and seeks to apply them to the realities of economic, social, and political structures. The initial group of eighteen is interracial and interfaith.

DISC continues to meet monthly to pray, reflect on the gospel, entertain guest speakers, welcome visitors, and work on community action. We continue to experience the joy of friendships formed and nurtured. We are always looking to respect the dignity and strength of people as they experience difficult times.

CHAPTER FOUR

ORGANIZING

LEADERSHIP TEAMS

Before exploring the wild and crazy world of organizing leadership teams, let's spend some time on what being a leader means. It is, in my opinion, the ability of a parish to surface, organize, and train leaders that will ultimately determine the success and effectiveness of its social ministry effort. As I reflect on my own past experience as a parish social ministry diocesan director, an essential question that was in constant need of attention was "What exactly is a parish leader or potential leader?"

The following "Rambling Reflections" are offered as one person's attempt to make some sense of that question about leadership. Please accept these as one perspective on a critical topic that should be discussed by each parish's core pastoral team.

RAMBLING REFLECTIONS ON LEADERS

First and foremost, a leader must be distinguished from a "doer." At the parish level, a doer is the person who, for whatever reason (and there are many) simply wants to "do" the ministry. She or he wants only to deliver the food basket, or visit a sick parishioner, or write a letter to a legislator, or be "a warm body" at the community action to close down a crack house. She or he does not understand the need (or chooses not to participate in the necessary planning and strategizing) for ongoing, efficient parish social ministry. Let's be clear, leaders "do" ministry. However, their main job is to organize opportunities for others to act, to find others to act, and then, through example and by generating inspiration, to challenge them to act.

A leader, while contemplating the need for action, will automatically (or with minimal prodding) think about and figure out how to get more people involved in the ministry. The true mark of a leader is that she or he has or can find followers.

A leader sees the big picture of social ministry and understands that "doing good" in the name of the parish does not just happen. As previously claimed, it requires:

▸ good *planning;*

▸ *coordination* within the parish, and, at times, with other parishes and congregations;

▸ accurate, consistent, and *regular communication* with the entire parish in a way that reinforces our call at baptism;

▸ relentlessly *inviting* and *recruiting* the rest of the parish to participate and contribute (in the broadest sense);

▸ *People! People! People* that can be counted on to deliver;

▸ *enthusiasm* and energy, driven by a desire for justice with action based on clear values for the long haul.

These requirements describe a particular "outlook" to social ministry an effective leader must have or develop. Personal qualities, such as being energetic, a good communicator, someone who is reasonably well organized, and so forth, that are most often attributed to leaders are helpful and woven within my proposed key qualities. However, for me, the starting point for effective leadership is the way a person views and then carries out her or his role as leader.

I rambled to now ask and address the following: "How does one go about organizing a team (committee) of leaders?" There are approximately ten steps for doing this. Those steps are offered as if the organizing process is beginning from scratch. There may be an existing group that is in disarray. If that is the case, simply review the steps, determine what has been missed, where the group currently is, and go from there. The steps are as follows:

▸ Find a few (three to five) allies who have a similar desire to get some organized ministry going. Convene the group.

▸ At that first gathering, talk about what you want to do and why. However, before moving forward with any action steps, remind yourselves that it will be wise and most constructive to invest some time in establishing the infrastructure of the team. A firm foundation early on will prevent a lot of chaos later. This will be difficult, as most leaders will have a strong desire to act. Have some patience. Engaging in action before you are ready may be fulfilling in the short term, but the team will likely fall apart or fizzle later. Remember that you are the leaders at this point, not the doers. BE SMART. Search your own experience—you know I'm right about this, don't you?

▸ Complete a parish analysis. (Use the "Parish Analysis Worksheet" on p. 57.) Spend some time getting to know the parish or community: its structure, how decisions are made, its key players, and its history. Do this as a group by dividing the parts of the worksheet and assigning specific responsibilities (See Session III, p. 75).You are finished and ready for step four when the worksheet is completed, remembering that much of the worksheet must be completed outside the meeting itself. Take your time with this. Stay focused.

▸ Clarify the specific purpose and function of the team. This is done by reviewing the vision and mission described earlier. That will serve as the context or umbrella under which the team exists. The team will probably be focusing on one of the ministry areas (direct service, legislative advocacy, global justice and peace efforts and global solidarity, or community organizing). However, it may have a different focus, such as adult education or recruitment (as described in the next section). You may also desire to have a team that is solely organized to serve as a coordinator for all the social ministry teams in the parish. You will know you are finished with this step when each member of the team can clearly articulate the purpose and special work of the team to any fellow parishioner and be understood.

Then you are ready to clarify the structure of the team, such as . . .

▸ How the team is going to operate (ground rules and decision-making);
▸ Leadership roles, especially the convener and the recorder;
▸ How often the team meets;
▸ How the team relates to the rest of the parish.

IMPORTANT SAFETY TIP: Do not get legalistic in this step. We are not trying to construct by-laws. We just want to establish some orderly way to conduct business. Common sense is always the guiding force. The whole thing can be finished in an hour.

Fill out the team by recruiting members. Anywhere from five to thirty members is workable, but eight to twelve is the norm. Having a clear purpose, function, and structure should make the team attractive. Potential members will get a sense of confidence in the group. When that happens, YOU'VE GOT THEM RIGHT WHERE YOU WANT THEM! More important, you have them right where Jesus wants them. How can they say no? (But don't be discouraged if they do!)

Orient the new members to the group and spend two or three sessions training all the members in the theological/scriptural roots of social ministry. Contact the diocesan Catholic Charities, Social Action Office, or Religious Education Office to either offer the sessions or help you organize them.

As a group, decide on one, two, or three projects the team will do over the next year. (Whew, FINALLY GOT TO THE ACTION. Now, however, you are ready for the long haul!) Make sure the action is well planned:

▸ Is each project divided into specific, concrete steps?
▸ Is it clear who has responsibility for what steps?

▶ Are the steps strategic (i.e., in line with what the team is capable of doing, and focused on an area that will get the maximum results)?

▶ Is there a strategy for getting more parishioners involved? (See the next section on recruitment.)

Periodically, but at least annually, evaluate the effort.

▶ What was accomplished and why?

▶ What was not accomplished and why?

▶ What changes or adjustments need to be made and why?

Celebrate the work, especially by thanking the Holy Spirit.

You've just taken an Intro to Organizing course, except for one thing. Don't forget to pray, both individually and collectively, all the while you are doing this. God expects a lot but will never get us into anything we cannot do if we just ask for the help!

RECRUITING

LEADERS

I t is my opinion that, except for prayer, recruiting leaders is the most important of the nine elements. Unless a parish is successful in generating volunteers, action on the full mission is not possible. Period! Exclamation point! End of story! It is as simple as that. (What I am about to say does not apply to you, but, instead, to all the OTHER parish ministers out there. So don't get defensive!)

The irony is that most parish ministers know this. They are always on the lookout for those illusive leaders. In addition, they are always complaining about parishioners not caring. They are always talking about getting new people involved but never doing it. They are always going to the same folks because "if you want something done, ask a busy person." WRONG! WRONG! WRONG!

As I get older (which is happening at an alarming rate), I am more and more convinced that the problem is with us. We fail to behave as if recruitment is the most important element of success. We are lazy about it! We tend to do it piecemeal and "occasional," when the need arises. To be successful, we must break out of that way of thinking and operating. When contemplating and doing recruitment of parishioners for social ministry efforts, we must, instead, be systematic and relentless. To be systematic means to have a specific plan. To be relentless means to be, well, relentless. Keep it going. Let's take a closer look at this issue.

Examine the following five scenarios and identify the one you believe to have the best chance of successfully recruiting people:

▸ There is an announcement in your parish bulletin requesting volunteers to join your parish social concerns committee.

▸ At Sunday Mass, Fr. Earl the Pearl gives a brief description of the parish social concerns committee and announces a need for volunteers. He tells people to see him if they are interested in joining.

35

▸ Same as above. However, Fr. Earl directs people to the table in the back where the social concerns committee member is seated and can answer questions and sign up volunteers.

▸ A member of the social concerns committee calls someone directly and asks her or him to join the committee.

▸ A member of the social concerns team calls someone previously identified from an individual visited by the "parish home visiting team" as a potential leader and invites that person to join a specific social ministry action or project or even the team.

Obviously, the last scenario has the best chance of success. It must be pointed out, however, that each one, more or less, has been used to successfully recruit volunteers. However, the last one is, by far, the best. It is a step in a broader process of parish community building that involves a one-on-one visit where a bond between the parish and the individual or family has been established. Asking someone to join something who has a sense of connection is always easier and holds a higher possibility for success. The key is the one-on-one home visit. The key is being relational, meeting a person face to face. A carpenter could be sitting in a congregation when the priest announces that the parish needs bookshelves. That carpenter could easily say to herself, "I sure hope someone comes through and buys bookshelves for the parish." A personal visit to that carpenter might help her see that she could build them, that her gifts, talents, and her very person are wanted and needed by the community. It's not that she is bad or lazy, she just didn't think of it. A personal relationship makes all the difference. Agree? If so, then how do we get there? Let's take a look.

HOME VISITS:
ONE SYSTEMATIC RECRUITMENT PROCESS

One period of time during a year, a specific number of home visits are conducted. (I recommend either the six weeks starting the first week of October and ending prior to Thanksgiving or the six weeks of Lent. However, any six weeks can be used.) The purpose of the visit is threefold:

▸ To generate a sense of energy and good will among parishioners;

▸ To listen for parish and community concerns, strengths, and visions;

▸ To identify potential ministry leaders and "doers" (BUT NOT RECRUIT THEM DURING THE VISIT).

The process has six steps, with an ever important seventh:

1. Organize a team of five to twenty "visitors." Their simple task is to visit one or two parishioners per week for five weeks.

2. This team should be separate from the social concerns committee. Social concerns committee members can be on the team, but the task of the team is straightforward and clear: to conduct home visits. It is different from the

job of the social concerns committee. When the job is done for the year, the team goes into hibernation until it is time to start again the following year. It is very important, though, for this team to be resurrected each year. (Relentless, remember?) Within three years, anywhere from 150 to 300 parishioners will be visited. Imagine the spirit, not to mention the pool of potential volunteers!

3. Train the visitors on how to make the visit. (See "Making the Visit" on p. 59.)

4. Select and distribute the names of the parishioners to be visited. *NOTE: Be creative in identifying parishioners who might be visited. Look to places like newly registered parishioners, members of small faith groups, seniors, youth, RCIA participants, etc. Remember that the purpose is to get beyond the usual suspects.*

5. Make the visit. Fill out the record form. (See "Parish Visitation Record" on p. 61.) Turn the forms into the social concerns committee chair. The summaries are scanned for potential leaders and/or persons who may be interested in getting involved in social ministry. The social concerns committee can now do some follow-up recruiting.

6. Have a "visitors" celebration/get-together. Talk about the experience. What were some of the concerns raised? What new parish assets were discovered? In general, how did it go? HOLD ON THERE, PARTNER . . . This is a time to talk about the experience and what was learned. IT IS NOT A TIME TO GOSSIP! Do not use specific names, please. We want people to trust us, don't we?

7. Congratulate yourselves on a job well done. Have some fun. Take a moment to thank the Holy Spirit for guiding you!

From the point of view of recruitment, this process is primarily used to find those people who will be leaders. That is, those people who will plan the efforts and, more important, call, invite, and recruit others to participate (the doers).

I have not found the magical, easy way to recruit participation in social ministry. I have witnessed parishes who have been able to generate one thousand volunteers, though. The only way to do it, as has been previously stated, is to be systematic and relentless in the approach.

CHAPTER SIX

SOCIAL

ANALYSIS

There is a marvelous parish-based, transformative educational process promoted by the Catholic Campaign for Human Development and, recently, in partnership with Catholic Charities USA called the "Journey to Justice" process. This formation-action effort starts with participants spending a weekend learning about the church's "Preferential Option for/with the Poor" in a very special, concrete way. The first step of the weekend journey is an intellectual exploration of the concept. The process then drives through and across scriptural pathways; accelerates and culminates into a powerful and inspiring immersion experience with an empowered low-income group. The retreat experience then decelerates with reflection on social sin and reconciliation and in learning the skill of social analysis. It is during the social analysis portion of the experience that questions about why the problems addressed by the low-income group exist in the community. The participants connect serious issues in their communities with the values of faith. They learn why the issues exist and how our Christian tradition can guide loving responses to those issues. It is a very powerful experience. (See p. 104 for more on Journey to Justice.)

It seems to me that social ministry at its best always includes an opportunity for all those involved to spend some time digging deeper into the problems that are being addressed. It is not enough to simply think a community problem exists. It is necessary to know the different ramifications and contributing causes of it. As a people of faith, it is also important to discern to what our religious tradition calls us by way of action. When ministers engage in a process that helps in their understanding of why a situation endures and how it is connected both to other community problems AND faith values, those ministers have a fuller and richer experience. The skill needed to engage in such activity is social analysis. The recommended social analysis vehicle is the "Pastoral Circle."

The "Pastoral Circle" was developed by Peter Henriot and Joe Holland and articulated in their book, *Social Analysis: Linking Faith and Justice* (Orbis Books). It has four components:

▸ Experiencing and describing a specific reality/concern/issue

▸ Social Analysis

▸ Theological/scriptural reflection

▸ Action as a result of that reflection

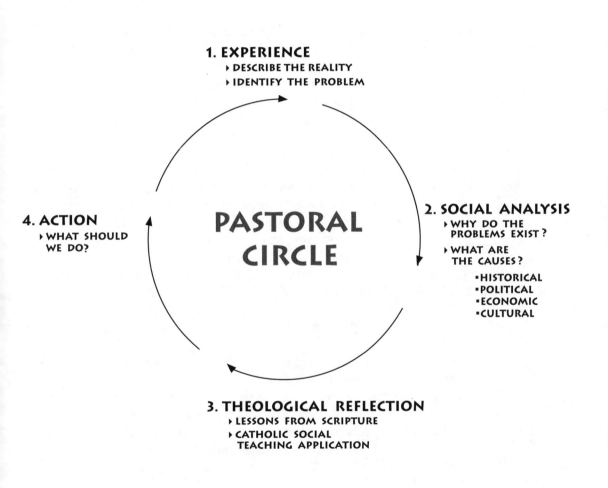

1. EXPERIENCE
  ▸ DESCRIBE THE REALITY
  ▸ IDENTIFY THE PROBLEM

4. ACTION
  ▸ WHAT SHOULD
    WE DO?

PASTORAL CIRCLE

2. SOCIAL ANALYSIS
  ▸ WHY DO THE
    PROBLEMS EXIST?
  ▸ WHAT ARE
    THE CAUSES?
      ▪HISTORICAL
      ▪POLITICAL
      ▪ECONOMIC
      ▪CULTURAL

3. THEOLOGICAL REFLECTION
  ▸ LESSONS FROM SCRIPTURE
  ▸ CATHOLIC SOCIAL
    TEACHING APPLICATION

Before suggesting a specific exercise meant to drive home the skill of using the pastoral circle, lets consider a brief side trip. Take another look at the four components of the pastoral circle. Like much of what is, hopefully, contained within the covers of this book, the pastoral circle is a disciplined, systematic application of everyday, homegrown logic. The pastoral circle is a process that starts with gathering all the objective information we have about a situation, issue, or problem. We address our own feelings about the problem and attempt to clarify the feelings of those experiencing the problems. The process then brings us to ask why the situation exists, and it pushes us to examine those reasons through the lens of our Catholic tradition, scripture, and our faith values. Finally, our faith guides the development of strategies for action. Then the cycle begins again as we assess, evaluate, and reflect on the consequences of those actions.

Try this image, if you will, to underscore the pastoral circle process . . . Have you ever watched really little kids run bases after hitting the ball (once they've figured out the correct direction to run)? They run like crazy, as fast as their little legs will carry them, to first base, stopping there with a screeching halt, no matter how far the ball is hit. They check things out before firing up the afterburners and rocketing to second base. Again, there is a flying STOP long enough to survey the situation. Once confident that it is safe to proceed, they move on, stopping at third. A final mad dash to home culminates in a slide (that is generally AFTER they've touched home plate) and a score. The base path ritual is repeated but is different each time because the game changes with every score. And, (this is the great part) it is always fun! This is the pastoral circle! Starting at the very beginning, each step (base) calls for a certain assessment before madly dashing to the next level. The final result is the completed action (score) that changes the game. (Everything we need to know about life can be found in a baseball game. It is even clearer when we watch little kids play it!)

PASTORAL CIRCLE
EXERCISE:

Set aside a meeting or two with your team to engage in this exercise. *(This activity could also be done in smaller segments over the course of three to five meetings.)* Using the "Pastoral Circle Worksheet" found on p. 63, select an issue, problem, or concern your team is confronting. For example, you may select "hunger" because your parish has a food pantry and regularly receives requests for food. Have each member of the team complete the worksheet. Then discuss the responses. After winding your way through the completion of the worksheet and subsequent discussions, the result should be a deeper understanding of the issue your team is addressing as well as a clearer perspective on why it is important, from a faith perspective, to be engaged in action to address it.

Please try to remember that this exercise is not meant to turn immediately into action. Its primary purpose is to help the participants get a deeper, fuller understanding of all aspects of a social ministry issue haunting the parish and the broader community. The action responses should be inserted into the regular planning process as described earlier in the chapter on the key elements of successful social ministry in the parish.

The pastoral circle process, with its four steps of *Experience*, *Analysis*, *Theological Reflection*, and *Action*, provides a tool for moving our faith into action in a way that ensures the greatest potential for success. It brings the depth that makes the effort really count. It helps us to take calculated, meaningful action in a way that keeps faith front and center. I recommend using this exercise often, with the wide variety of social issues that you will encounter.

ⅴ GREAT PARISHES,
ⅠⅠ GREAT IDEAS

Here's an example of a parish that used social analysis to effectively serve the people.

ST. FRANCIS OF ASSISI PARISH

Diocese of Baltimore, Maryland

Rev. Bill Burke, Pastor

Sr. Kate Bell, R.S.M., Pastoral Associate

(Reflections written by Sr. Kate Bell, R.S.M.)

St. Francis of Assisi Parish identified a need to respond to the people in the community who were being impacted by the recent welfare reform effort. After meeting several times about the issue with other churches and community groups, the parish decided on a creative approach that combines the compassion of direct service and the broad scope of community-based development. The "Loan Up" program was born. This program provides critical capital to low-income people who need funds to begin or complete their transition from unemployment or welfare to work. It works to install a sense of dignity in the lives of those participating in it. The loan recipients work to pay back the money so that the funds can go to others in the targeted community.

The "Loan Up" strategy is to replace the traditional handout with a debt instrument that will be paid back over a defined period at 0% interest. The funds are reserved for activities or expenses directly related to one's moving from welfare to work. The funds do not cover emergency assistance but will cover things like training, uniform purchase, auto repair, etc. Loans are worked through participating banks. In all, this has proved to be a creative, productive new ministry.

CHAPTER SEVEN

INTEGRATING AND

COORDINATING

THE PARISH SOCIAL

MINISTRY EFFORT

A common phenomenon is for parish social ministry to become disconnected from the rest of the parish. We have all seen it happen. A small group of well-intentioned social activists lay claim to the social justice mission of the parish congregation and go chariot racing off into the sunset leaving the rest of the parish in their dust. Or, conversely, the parish pastoral leadership fails to remember that social ministry is as important to the living out of our faith as celebrating the eucharist, that eucharist becomes fulfilling only to the extent that those receiving are, in turn, inspired to go out into the world to love their neighbor. Consequently, those members of the parish who firmly believe in social ministry are forced to practically run a clandestine operation.

I have only one thing to say about both cases: "STOP IT! Start playing well together or we'll have to make you stay in a room staring at each other until you see one another's Christ-likeness!" Social ministry is at the heart of who we are as a people of faith. Scripture tells us so. The example of Jesus tells us so. Catholic social teaching tells us so. The innocent, child-like faith each of us has deep within our hearts that gets expressed in commonsense, everyday moral decisions tells us so. Everyone has a right and responsibility to engage in it. It does belong in parish life and not just to a few but to all the baptized. Parish social ministry as described in these reflections is just an organized, systematic way of doing it.

43

It cannot be disconnected from the rest of the parish and be forthright or, as important, wholly effective. How then, does it stay connected? How is it coordinated? Refer to the "Parish Social Ministry Integration Examination of Conscience Exercise" found on page 66.

One final word on this topic of integration. For five years, my family and I lived in a very small, vibrant, inner city parish. The parish was certainly not wealthy. Its parishioners could be found in the "working class to poor" economic and social categories. It was not one of those parishes where there were a lot of suburbanites coming in from the outer reaches because of a charismatic pastor. It was just a solid, simple parish committed to all aspects of parish life, including social ministry outreach. We had a number of small social ministry leadership teams, which did a great deal of work. A lot of parish-based social ministry was accomplished. Parishioners were well informed of these activities and hundreds of people in a 400-family parish were connected, in one way or another. Their involvement was not always at the leadership level, but certainly they were contributors to the extent their time, skill, and interest allowed. Occasionally, persons both volunteered to serve while, at the same time, they received aid.

I share this nostalgic side trip to St. Anthony Parish in Southern Indiana to say that good integration, coordination of, and involvement in parish social ministry has nothing to do with financial resources. As I said, we were a relatively poor parish. Instead, it has everything to do with will and commitment. It has nothing to do with a magnetic, superstar leader. Instead, it has everything to do with caring, mature, disciplined, and empowering leadership (which the St. Anthony pastoral team possessed in abundance).

In other words, I do not want anyone to read this and say something like, "Well you can do this if you live in a large, well-financed parish who has the perfect pastor." Thanks to my beloved St. Anthony Parish, I can say with the confidence that comes from lived experience, it "just ain't so."

Being well organized, having a clear vision, and having a simple plan to build that vision has nothing to do with financial resources. It has nothing to do with charismatic pastors. The wealthiest parishes as well as the poorest ones have an equal chance at providing solid, effective care for and with the "least" among us. It takes inspiration from the Holy Spirit, solid and empowered leaders, patience, and a disciplined approach to providing that care. Oh, and of course, a really great sense of humor!

CHAPTER EIGHT

PARTNERS IN CRIME:

THE DIOCESE

AND THE PARISH

(WHY A RELATIONSHIP BETWEEN THE DIOCESE AND A PARISH IS A GOOD THING)

Once upon a time, there was a diocesan department that provided emergency services to, for, and with low-income individuals and families. After some time, the diocesan staff observed that there were a number of people coming to them in need of free or low cost legal services. A department board member, who was a sympathetic private attorney, was approached about the possibility of providing pro bono services. He not only agreed, but also helped to develop an elaborate plan to recruit fellow attorneys to join him in his volunteer efforts. Further, it was decided by the planners to use parishes as the base of their generous, useful efforts. Numerous parishes were contacted to come to a meeting where "the plan" would be unveiled. Everyone was pleased and ready to live happily ever after, except for one minor, little, tiny thing. It did not work!

This true scenario failed initially because no one took the time to bring parish representatives into the planning process. The way the initiative was first envisioned did not take into consideration several parish issues. As a result, the parishes were, at best, lukewarm to the idea.

There is a happy ending, though. The moment the diocesan office and the parishes agreed to come together to figure out the project, keeping the needs of each in mind, the program flourished. It is a huge success to this day. This situation and its resolution taught me a lot about the partnership between parishes and other organizations, especially Catholic Charities agencies and other Catholic diocesan offices.

In my professional life, and at times in my personal life, I have walked in two worlds: social ministry at the diocesan level (through Catholic Charities agencies) and at the parish level. To me, parishes and agencies are at their very best when there is a strong, positive relationship between the two. (Something that was eventually achieved in the above case study, but was a missing piece in the beginning.) Such a relationship is not a requirement for social ministry to occur, but it does need to be present if the highest and most useful levels of ministry are to be attained.

I have always thought this kinship between Catholic Charities agencies or the diocese and parishes is as natural as baseball season starting in the spring. (Again, all of life is a simple reflection of the ebbs and flows of a baseball season, but that, alas, is a different—although fascinating—topic.) Perhaps it all seems so obvious to me, and I can seem to be far too hopeful at times. As my family often asks, "Does your balloon ever land?" In other words, as natural as those linkages may seem to me, they are often very difficult to achieve.

Countless times I hear dedicated diocesan representatives lament the uncooperative, overly demanding dispositions of parish people, especially pastors. Parishes, on the other hand, express similar disdain, commenting that agencies see parishes only as exploitable pools of volunteers and repositories of diocesan-mandated programs that have little to do with parish needs, desires, or realities. It seems to me that both points of view are honest and, often times, accurate. That, however, does not have to be and should not be the case.

The starting point for a healthy relationship is the commonsense understanding that there are mutual self-interests involved; that locating the common ground is the essence of playing well together. It requires an empathic understanding of each other's realities. When such mutual respect is in operation, the door opens to focusing on the broader needs of the community.

From this point of reference, a strong, constructive partnership can be built. These guiding principles, which can be applied to either or both perspectives (parish and diocesan), are recommended:

▸ Be clear about your own mission. Know what your parish or diocesan agency's focus is. Communicate that early and often. Do not be arrogant or rigid about it. Just be confident in it. The more you are in touch with your own social ministry purpose and able to clearly state it, the better.

▸ Learn something about the other by spending a little time with them. Through an individual meeting, learn who is in charge, how decisions are made, on what efforts most of the resources are expended, what the primary interests and values of those in charge are, and what the organizational structure is.

▸ In a sincere manner, and with integrity, attempt to fit your mission and interests with the other's. Determine if there is a real fit. Do not try to change either. Articulate your purpose and mission in language that reflects the other's interests. For example, if a diocesan office's mission calls for a legal aid network, the interests of the parish must be understood. The network should help the parish as well as the diocesan office. The missions and goals must be compatible. The time used to determine this is time well spent.

- "Make an offer they can't refuse." The diocese can offer consultation time (to help with planning and execution), resources such as education material, training activities, and networking opportunities. The parish can provide people and proximity to the action. However, both make the offer only when each is satisfied that mutual interests will be met.

- Establish a "contract." An agreement, usually verbal, is reached that states that each can be counted on to deliver what was offered.

- Monitor the relationship on an ongoing basis.

- Celebrate and affirm the relationship on a regular basis.

- Now, go out and play!

CHAPTER NINE

BEING A GOOD

FACILITATOR

The following is offered in the shadow of well-intentioned but too long and unfocused meetings that make each of us tired all over. Worse, those meetings make us dread team gatherings, thinking the only good thing is that we will go straight to heaven because we surely have already suffered through purgatory. You know exactly what I am talking about, don't you? They appear out of nowhere and lurk in every church basement. There you are, sitting with a few team members, chatting but keeping all your really great and potentially "savior-esque" ideas ready in anticipation of the start of the meeting. Then the meeting never quite comes to order. It never quite gets focused. The participants never quite know what the next step is. Many "idea planes" take off but never quite land. Two hours and fifteen minutes later, everyone is exhausted and the meeting ends. The next date is set and most of the people silently plan to be busy, even if it means cleaning the bathroom on that next date. Anything is better than sitting through one of those again.

Now, I'm sure that none of YOU has ever been responsible for that sort of meeting. Therefore, the hints for facilitation (the little things that will stave off such a disastrous event) which follow are meant for all those OTHER potential leaders out there who also happen to be really poor facilitators. It should be noted that the list found on page 68 was compiled during a recent meeting with my Catholic Charities USA colleges on the topic of being a good facilitator. In addition, there are numerous excellent resources on this topic. I recommend getting a hold of some of those (take a look at the resources mentioned on page 70). Photocopy "Some Direction for Facilitators" on page 68 for the entire team. Sharpening facilitator skills is definitely worth doing. A well-facilitated meeting, even on topics of little interest, will always be a successful one. I guarantee it!

FINALLY

A few years ago, we had a small, two-door car. In order to comfortably climb into the rear seat, the passenger had to push a foot pedal, which, in turn, made the front seat lean forward. The foot pedal had a small rubber covering on it. Unfortunately, at some point, the rubber covering came off. I decided to put it back on. This was during a very warm summer, and getting the thing back on was a difficult, cramped maneuver. Have you ever tried to put a plastic lid onto a container that is slightly too large? You push it down on one side and it pops up on the other. That's what it was like. It took me about forty-five minutes, with lots of sweat, and a cuss word or two.

That same afternoon, I was driving somewhere with my wife and my loving but very pitiful son who was thirteen years old at the time. While in the car, I was lamenting my poor mechanical skills by whining about—I mean—describing the extremely difficult time I had in doing the simple repair job of putting that stupid rubber covering back on the foot pedal. I was especially emphasizing my frustration and embarrassment at being such a lousy mechanic. At that moment, my son, enthusiastically and with great encouragement shouted, "Oh no, Dad, you did a great job! I had to yank real hard to pull it off." I turned to see his smiling, reassuring face with the small rubber covering held up in front of it. Stunned, I looked at my wife, then back to my son. My always-sympathetic wife simply shook her head and said, "That's your child!"

I have a point in telling this story beyond embarrassing my son. Learning life's lessons from my kids, even the teenagers, has become a way of living for me. This situation had, for me, a valuable hidden message. It always struck me that the primary motivation for my well-intentioned, enthusiastic son was passionate kindness, regardless of the consequences. It seems to me, the first and most important ingredient for a successful parish social minister is passionate kindness. That is what our brother Jesus was all about, and he calls his followers to nothing less. At the same time, our passionate kindness must be disciplined, well thought out, and efficient if we are to truly help bring about God's reign.

This book has been, at its heart, about passionate kindness. While we spent time with some practical things, such as doing parish surveys, interviewing parishioners, and running meetings, we were all the while about the business of bringing about God's reign. Nothing less will do. I firmly believe that this happens through parish-based social ministry. I believe it happens through organizing others and offering a discipline to people's desire to help. This book has been an attempt to assist with that discipline. I hope it has been helpful, and in keeping with my son's instruction, not overly boring.

I'll be standing with you as we all seek to do as the Lord has told us: act justly, love tenderly, and walk humbly with our God. Please, please, please, in the process, remember to celebrate. Or I will have to make you sit out an inning with me in the dugout. My son will tell you, you don't want that.

My next book will be all about ministry and life's lessons learned from baseball.

PART TWO

WORKSHEETS AND RESOURCES
FOR EFFECTIVE
PARISH SOCIAL MINISTRY

Part One covered many questions about parish social ministry, and I attempted to answer them. Part Two provides some of the material that will be helpful in your work. I have provided some worksheets to accompany the chapters in Part One, as well as some sample agendas for social concerns committee meetings, background material on Catholic social teaching, contact information for some helpful folks, and some other resources that you might find useful. Please remember that your situation is unique, so take what I offer and adjust it to fit your needs. There is sometimes a danger in offering resources and ideas. That danger is that they are taken as the only way to do this work. Don't let any of this limit you in your creativity. Use the resources only as they are helpful to you.

PARISH SOCIAL MINISTRY
SUCCESS WORKSHEET

THE CONTEXT . . .

The following is a checklist or "examination of parish social ministry conscience" designed to provide a self-evaluation of your parish social ministry effort. It is based on experience that indicates that if your parish social ministry activities involve a significant portion of these "elements of success," it will be very productive.

It is recommended that this instrument be completed, discussed, and analyzed by a core team of parish social ministry leaders. However, it has proven to be a helpful exercise even if an individual leader or staff person uses it.

THE INSTRUCTIONS . . .

Rate the extent to which your social ministry effort incorporates each element of success by placing a number in the space provided. (0 = my parish social ministry does not have this element; 1 to 4 = my parish social ministry effort includes this element of success, more or less; 5 = my parish social ministry effort completely includes this element of success.) Use the questions under each element to guide your understanding of the element and, therefore, rate the extent to which it is a part of your social ministry work.

THE INSTRUMENT . . .

To what extent is your parish social ministry effort . . .

Linked to faith? _____

Do the leaders regularly reflect on scripture and Catholic social teaching and discuss how the social ministry effort is an expression of faith in action?

Is the social mission woven into parish worship?

COMMENTS/ANALYSIS:

Clear on how it will bring about a more just world? _____

Do the leaders understand how their efforts are helping to bring about the reign of God?
COMMENTS/ANALYSIS:

Touching a system of values? _____

Do participants feel strongly that what they are doing is right and just?

Is there a sense of just (productive) anger present?
COMMENTS/ANALYSIS:

Focused, addressing the full mission of social ministry? _____

Is there a realistic plan that includes some specific strategies involving direct service, legislative advocacy, and community organizing guiding the social ministry effort?
COMMENTS/ANALYSIS:

Providing leaders with an opportunity to explore the deeper social, political, and institutional causes of the problems being addressed? _____
COMMENTS/ANALYSIS:

Taken from *Parish Social Ministry: Strategies for Success* by Tom Ulrich © 2001 by Ave Maria Press, Inc.
Used with permission. All rights reserved.

Recruiting leaders in an ongoing, systematic way? _____

Does the plan include a vehicle that intentionally identifies and recruits several new persons onto the parish social ministry leadership team every year?

COMMENTS/ANALYSIS:

Developing the leadership team? _____

Are skills-building training sessions available for the team?

Are all the available parish social ministry resources known?

COMMENTS/ANALYSIS:

Known and supported by the whole parish? _____

Is there regular reporting to the pastor and pastoral team?

Is there a regular communication system in place that informs the entire parish about the parish social ministry activities?

Are parishioners invited to join specific parish social ministry actions and reminded of their baptismal call to social ministry?

COMMENTS/ANALYSIS:

Involving the people experiencing the problems? _____

Are there opportunities for those experiencing the problems (e.g., poor people, women who have had abortions, etc.) to speak their minds and be listened to?

Are those experiencing the problems recruited as leaders and/or involved in actions?

COMMENTS/ANALYSIS:

THE ANALYSIS . . .

Based on your ratings:

Identify your parish social ministry's primary strengths.

Identify two or three key areas you want to improve.

STRATEGIC PLANNING . . .

Based on your analysis, identify three or four tasks your team will tackle next year:

PARISH ANALYSIS WORKSHEET

PARISH INFORMATION

Parish _____ Deanery/Region/Grouping _____

Number of Parishioners _____ Number of Families _____

Average Family Income _____ Average Weekly Collection _____

Catholic Campaign for Human Development Collection _____

Catholic Relief Services Operation Rice Bowl Collection _____

Ethnic Makeup _____

Pastor's Longevity _____ Number of Priests _____

Number of Parish Staff Members (include deacons)_____

Number of Parish Social Ministry Volunteers _____

OPEN QUESTIONS

PARISH:

What are the key issues/concerns currently in the parish?

What are the noteworthy organizations in the parish?

What significant programs are currently taking place in the parish (e.g., RENEW, Stewardship, etc)?

PASTOR:

What are his main parish concerns or issues?

Does he have any special interests?

How would you describe his leadership style?

PARISH DECISION-MAKING & STRUCTURE:

How are decisions at the parish made? Who has influence?

How would you describe the parish structure?

OTHER COMMENTS/OBSERVATIONS:

Rate the Parish Social Ministry Effort (High/Medium/Low):

	CURRENT	POTENTIAL
Direct Service		
Public Policy		
Advocacy		
Justice & Peace/Global Solidarity		
CCHD & CRS		
Community		
Organizing		

PRE-VISIT:

This visit is a relatively brief conversation where the home visitor primarily listens to a fellow parishioner's concerns, vision, and listing of parish and community strengths. It should be prearranged, probably by telephone.

SAMPLE APPOINTMENT CALL:

"Hello! My name is _____ and I am a member of the home visiting team at _____ parish. We are visiting families in our parish community to listen to their point of view and ideas regarding the parish and the community. Could I arrange to have about thirty or forty minutes of your time to visit with you?"

THE VISIT:

▸ Introduce yourself again and explain why you are there.

▸ Begin the conversation with some questions about the person's family. Move on to exploring their thoughts on parish and community issues and strengths (what should be fixed and what is working well). Also ask what they think the parish or community ought to look like (their vision).

▸ Use follow-up questions for more detail, to stimulate the conversation, and for your own curiosity about something said. Be sure to ask a lot of "why" questions.

REMEMBER . . . you are there to listen, not to talk about your pet projects, sell them on anything, or to recruit them (although a question about what their interests are, as far as involvement is concerned, can and should be asked). If the person asks questions about the parish that you do not know, indicate that and let them know you will be happy to refer them or their question to the appropriate person.

POST-VISIT:

When the visit is completed, spend a few minutes filling out the report form. Do not fill it out during the visit, but do not wait too long. The visit should be fresh when the form is completed.

INTERVIEW
IDEAS

In conducting the interview, keep the following in mind as helpful conversation starters. They also serve to identify needs in the parish.

FAMILY

Kids (ages, grade levels, gender, involvement)

Schools

Hopes for kids

Concerns for kids

Employment (where, how long, enjoy it?)

Roots

Unique pressures faced by families

How do you have fun with your family?

PARISH

Feelings about the parish

Opinion about parish morale or spirit

Suggestions for change

Description of the ideal parish

Personal involvement

NEIGHBORHOOD/COMMUNITY

How long there

Changes over time . . . for better or worse?

Problems/concerns

Community strengths

Personal involvement in community activity

PARISH VISITATION
RECORD

DATE: _____

NAME (of person interviewed): _____

ADDRESS: _____

PHONE: _____

COMMENTS ABOUT PARISH

Specific Concerns:

COMMENTS ABOUT COMMUNITY

Specific Concerns:

VISITOR COMMENTS

(Could include: Other people whom they think should be interviewed; how you felt you did as an interviewer; any tensions felt in the interview, etc.)

Specific Concerns:

POTENTIAL LEADER: YES   NO

Interviewer: _____

Address: _____

Phone: _____

(Please add additional comments below)

PASTORAL CIRCLE
WORKSHEET

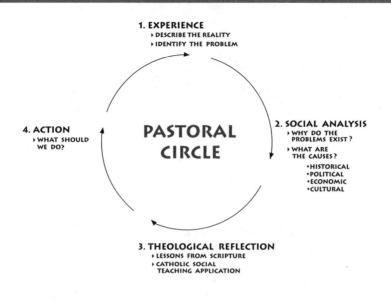

1. EXPERIENCE
‣ DESCRIBE THE REALITY
‣ IDENTIFY THE PROBLEM

PASTORAL CIRCLE

4. ACTION
‣ WHAT SHOULD WE DO?

2. SOCIAL ANALYSIS
‣ WHY DO THE PROBLEMS EXIST?
‣ WHAT ARE THE CAUSES?
  •HISTORICAL
  •POLITICAL
  •ECONOMIC
  •CULTURAL

3. THEOLOGICAL REFLECTION
‣ LESSONS FROM SCRIPTURE
‣ CATHOLIC SOCIAL TEACHING APPLICATION

The name of our issue/problem is _____ .

EXPERIENCE/REALITY:

What is going on at your parish regarding this issue? (Describe it as fully—with specific details—as possible.)

What are the feelings expressed by those experiencing the problem?

How do you feel as a result of the experience? How does this touch you personally?

SOCIAL ANALYSIS:

From what you know, why does this situation exist?

Political Factors (government policies, education policies, etc.)

Economic Factors (jobs, banking practices, etc.)

Historic Factors (earlier discrimination practices, etc.)

Social Factors (stereotypes and prejudices, etc.)

What are the reasons for the situation given by those experiencing the problem?

What groups in the community or diocese are addressing this situation (both direct services and social action)?

THEOLOGICAL REFLECTION:

What key principles or lessons from scripture and Catholic social teaching apply to this experience?

How, in your opinion, would Jesus address this experience?

ACTION RESPONSE:

Do you have enough information and analysis to act? If not, what additional research is needed?

How are the poor being empowered to address these problems themselves?

What actions might be undertaken to address and resolve the problem/issue?

PARISH SOCIAL MINISTRY INTEGRATION
EXAMINATION OF CONSCIENCE EXERCISE

This exercise asks the leadership team to spend a few minutes during a meeting completing and discussing the checklist. After identifying what your team is missing by way of integrating its effort into the rest of the parish, create a strategy to shore up the weaknesses.

▸ To what extent is there a system of regular communication (i.e., face-to-face meetings and written reports) between the parish pastoral leadership and the parish social ministry teams?

▸ Does that communication update and fully inform each party about activities taken and planned?

▸ To what extent is there regular reporting and integration of social ministry activities at liturgical celebrations and services?

▸ Bulletin/newsletter descriptions and clip art.

▸ Announcements at Mass.

▸ Weekly inclusion of social ministry work in the "Prayer of the Faithful."

▸ Regular connection of social ministry work in homilies and reflections.

▸ Social ministry recognition and commissioning during appropriate liturgies, such as Holy Thursday's washing of the feet.

▸ The activities of the Catholic Campaign for Human Development, Catholic Relief Services, and Respect Life described at their designated "season."

▸ Are there adult education and formation opportunities on Catholic social teaching provided (at least) during Advent and Lent?

▸ Are the Catholic Campaign for Human Development, Catholic Relief Services, and Respect Life materials distributed annually?

▸ Does the review for orthodoxy and selection of religious education materials used in the parish include adherence to the full teaching of Catholic social teaching as described in the *Catechism of the Catholic Church* and the U.S. Bishops' *Communities of Salt and Light*?

- Do small faith groups promoted and supported by the parish utilize material that has a social ministry action component?

- Does the parish pastoral council have a connection to the parish social ministry work being done in the name of the parish? (That connection can be either formal through a designated representative or informal through some type of reporting mechanism.)

- Do the social ministry team leaders have a regular (probably on a quarterly basis) meeting where efforts are described and celebrated and skills training is offered?

- Are all members of the parish invited to join the ministry in some manner, and on a continuing basis?

- Prayer networks given specific social ministry intentions to place on prayer lists.

- Bulletin invitation for joining specific ministry teams such as the St. Vincent de Paul Society, including whom to contact and how.

- Systematic and relentless recruitment strategy designed and implemented.

- Social ministry fairs are held on an annual basis where a designated Sunday Mass (usually in early Fall) includes an invitation for parishioners to visit with ministry team leaders stationed in the back of church or in the parish hall.

- Is the youth group connected to all social ministry teams with opportunities to do "community service" (especially if this is a school requirement)?

SOME DIRECTION
FOR FACILITATORS

Successful facilitators attend to five primary activities. They are:

1. Listen and clarify what you hear. Listen and clarify! Listen and clarify!

2. Stimulate discussion by posing focusing type questions.

3. Manage the conversation by directing the questions to the whole group, summarizing key points being made, and keeping track of the time.

4. Prior to the conversation, have a relatively clear but flexible plan for moving the flow of the discussion. *(Do not mistake this for having the answers to the questions or solutions to the problems. This must come from the group.)*

5. Listen and clarify! Listen and clarify! Listen and clarify! (Have I made my point?)

COMMON MISTAKES
FACILITATORS MAKE

▸ The facilitator interacts with only one person for long periods of time.

▸ The objectives for the discussion are unclear or nonexistent.

▸ There is an inconsistent time frame—starting late and ending late.

▸ The conversation is allowed to get off track.

▸ There is too much personal interjection. The facilitator presumes to have all the answers.

▸ Several conversations are going on at the same time.

▸ The facilitator assumes that the whole group is familiar with all the terms and language.

▸ Participants take criticizing positions.

▸ The meeting was thrown together; there was a lack of preparation.

▸ The rules changed in the middle; there is a hidden agenda.

▸ There is no order to people speaking.

▸ The facilitator does not have the needed materials.

▸ The facilitator allows a few people to dominate.

▸ There is an unclear agenda at the beginning; the facilitator does not state the meeting objectives up front.

▸ There is no closure to discussion.

Taken from *Parish Social Ministry: Strategies for Success* by Tom Ulrich © 2001 by Ave Maria Press, Inc.
Used with permission. All rights reserved.

SIMPLE FACILITATOR
GUIDELINES

▸ Engage the whole group.

▸ Create a clear agenda for the meeting and stick to it. A crisp agenda will always have a simple purpose with specific objectives.

▸ Start and end on time. Let me say that again. Start and end on time.

▸ Keep the conversation on track. Do not hesitate to bring it back to the topic at hand.

▸ Be disciplined and orderly but not oppressive.

▸ Constantly seek clarity; make few assumptions.

▸ Keep your opinions to yourself! Your job is to focus the opinions of others; stimulate discussion and create the atmosphere for making group decisions.

▸ Establish ground rules for the meeting discussion up front.

▸ Be aware of the general emotional state of the group; always have your "antennae" up.

▸ Recap what is said; keep the conversation moving.

▸ If called for, distribute follow-up tasks and responsibilities.

A SUGGESTION . . .

Like playing shortstop, developing into a competent, even expert, facilitator takes lots of practice. (I am still trying to fit that baseball analogy in somewhere.) A suggested exercise is to find someone you trust and ask them to observe your facilitation style over the course of a six-month period of time. Have that person use the above to critique your performance. From those sessions, identify specific areas to work on during each facilitation experience. Relax and have some fun!

FACILITATOR
RESOURCES

The best set of resources dealing with being an effective facilitator that I have encountered comes from a publishing company called Jossey-Bass. They specialize in organizational development issues and offer topnotch, wide-ranging resources. While they concentrate on corporate development, I have found that it is very easy to translate the material into the world of ministry.

The Jossey-Bass resource catalog can be obtained by calling them at 1-800-956-7739 or via the Internet at www.josseybass.com.

The most comprehensive resource on meeting facilitation that I have used and can recommend is:

The Skilled Facilitator: Practical Wisdom for Developing Effective Groups by Roger M. Schwarz. Jossey-Bass Publishers, Inc. (San Francisco), 1994.

ANOTHER WONDERFUL RESOURCE:

Facilitating With Ease! A Step-by-Step Guidebook With Customizable Worksheets on CD-ROM by Ingrid Bens. Jossey-Bass Publishers, Inc. (San Francisco), 2000.

It occurred to me that it might be useful to offer a series of "agendas" or work sessions a parish team could utilize in order to get itself organized to do social ministry as described in this book. What follows is such a series. They are presented in a sequence that is meant to build on the previous session, and they reflect a set of general organizing steps that will launch parish-based social ministry as it is envisioned. If you like, you can follow them in the order they are presented, like a cookbook. However, please, please, please, do not back away from your instincts to pick, choose, and make adjustments to order or content. Making your effort your own is always the best way to proceed (but then, you knew that already, didn't you?). Also, you may want to offer several sessions as a part of a daylong retreat. There are a number of ways to proceed, so be creative and think through what is right for your team.

My starting point in this activity is the assumption that there is a small but dedicated parish social concerns committee in existence that is trying to get itself organized, jump-started, or renewed. (If this does not exist, get such a team together, first. Use a variation of the recruitment techniques outlined in the section on recruiting leaders.) With this small (five to fifteen folks) but powerful (okay, at least enthusiastic) group of leaders, set aside three to six months to take the steps given using the session outlines provided.

(One side note worth considering): It may be helpful to have the team read the section of the book titled "Organizing Leadership Teams" (pp. 31-34) as preparation for this process.

SESSION I:

TEAM ROLE CLARIFICATION

SESSION OBJECTIVES:

1. To clarify the difference between a "leader" and a "doer."

2. To reinforce the role of the team as leaders, NOT doers.

OPENING (20 MINUTES):

1. Call session to order and introduce any new members.

2. State what the team is going to be doing over the next several months and why. This will provide the context and focus for the gatherings.

3. Present the session objectives.

4. Opening prayer.

CLARIFY DIFFERENCE BETWEEN "LEADER" & "DOER" (30 MINUTES):

1. Distribute copies of the first portion (from the beginning through "One Final Ramble") of the "Organizing Leadership Teams" section of the book. Read this individually.

2. Ask for clarifying questions.

3. Engage in a discussion about what the difference is between being a leader and a doer. These focus questions may help guide the discussion:

▸ In your own words, what is the difference between a leader and a doer? What are the main distinctions between the two?

▸ When in your life have you been a leader? A doer?

▸ What are the main motivations of a leader? How are they different from those of a doer?

▸ Can you think of ministries at our parish where a leader would be needed? A doer?

▸ What does a leader bring to ministry that is unique to that role? What uniquely does a doer bring?

CLARIFY THE ROLE OF THIS TEAM (20 MINUTES):

1. State that the role of this team is to be leaders, NOT doers. Your job is to find, recruit, and enable other members of the parish to get active in some component of the social ministry effort, NOT do the work yourself.

2. In light of the previous discussion, give participants a chance to react to this position. These focus questions may be helpful.

▶ Why is it important for this team to have as its primary function being leaders (and not doers)?

▶ At what point is it appropriate for the leaders of this team to also be doers?

3.   Get consensus on the role of the committee.

WRAP-UP (3 MINUTES):

1. Set the next meeting date.

2. Distribute copies of the chapter titled "Vision and Mission" (pp. 13-17) with instructions for team members to read it as homework for the next session.

3. Very brief closing prayer/reflection.

SESSION II:
UNDERSTANDING THE MISSION
OF PARISH SOCIAL MINISTRY

SESSION OBJECTIVES:

1. To understand the full vision and mission of parish social ministry.
2. To clarify the five major components of that vision.

OPENING (15 MINUTES, INCLUDING PRAYER):

1. Call the session to order.
2. Opening prayer.
3. Present the objectives.

UNDERSTANDING THE FULL VISION &
MISSION OF SOCIAL MINISTRY (60 MINUTES):

1. Read aloud the references from *Economic Justice for All* and Communities of *Salt and Light* that were in the reading assignment.

2. Ask participants the question(s): "What strikes you about the message conveyed in these passages?" "What is most meaningful to you?" (This should be a free-flowing sharing and is meant to give people an opportunity to express feelings about the content. However, do not let the conversation go longer than fifteen minutes.)

3. Have team members re-read chapter one, describing the vision, mission, and elements (pp. 13-17). Also, have them examine the descriptive chart that is provided. Discuss and analyze the content. You may want to use the following questions:

▸ Are there any clarifying questions you have?

▸ Can you restate the parish social ministry mission using your own words?

▸ What two or three things do you feel this mission is attempting to accomplish in the parish?

▸ What are specific examples of each of the ministry components?

▸ Why is this considered to be a "full" vision of parish-based social ministry? Why is it important to a parish to work toward offering a full vision of social ministry?

WRAP-UP (10 MINUTES):

1. Restate the session objectives and determine if they were accomplished.

2. Distribute a copy of the chapter titled "The Foundation of the Full Mission" (pp. 18-24) and ask participants to read it for the next session.

3. Set the meeting date for the next meeting.

4. Offer a closing prayer.

SESSION III:
RENEWING OUR
FOUNDATION IN FAITH

(If your team would like to pursue a comprehensive experience in social ministry formation, I strongly recommend that you review the description of JustFaith located in the description of Catholic Charities USA resources (p. 102). It is a proven method for generating both understanding of and enthusiasm for social ministry. You should seriously consider replacing this session with that experience. It would be well worth the time invested! If this route is chosen, please feel free to suspend the organizing of the team while you are doing this formation work. Again, it is well worth the investment!)

SESSION OBJECTIVES:

1. To clarify the difference between direct service and social action.

2. To discover the call to direct service and social action in Catholic social teaching and holy scripture.

OPENING
(15 MINUTES, INCLUDING PRAYER):

1. Call session to order.

2. Opening prayer.

3. Present the session objectives.

DIRECT SERVICE & SOCIAL ACTION
(30 MINUTES):

1. Read, discuss, and analyze the section identifying the characteristics of direct service and social action in the book's "The Foundation of the Full Mission" (pp. 18-24). You may want to utilize these focus questions:

▸ In your own words, what are the characteristics of direct service? Of social action?

▸ How are these two types of ministry different? How are they "woven together" as is claimed?

▸ When is it best to offer direct service ministry? When is it best to offer social action ministry?

▸ Why is direct service "ministry"? Why is social action "ministry"?

SCRIPTURE AND DIRECT SERVICE/SOCIAL ACTION MINISTRY
(30 MINUTES):

▸ Do the scripture reading exercise described on p. 20. Follow the instructions as provided.

**WRAP-UP
(15 MINUTES):**

1. Restate the session objectives and determine if they were accomplished.

2. Hand out copies of the "Parish Analysis Worksheet" found on p. 57.

▸   Divide the team into four research subgroups (one for each section of the worksheet: "Parish Information," "Open Questions: PARISH," "Open Questions: PASTOR," "Open Questions: PARISH DECISION-MAKING & STRUCTURE").

▸   Each subgroup is given the assignment to answer each of the questions in their particular area, bringing the subgroup's completed section to report at the next meeting. Remind participants that they may need to speak to the parish staff to get the information.

▸   Inform the pastor that your team is doing this research on the parish.

3. Set the next meeting date.

4. Offer a closing prayer.

SESSION IV:
SELF-ASSESSMENT

(The following session may take one to three meetings to accomplish. If it goes more than three, you are most likely being bogged down. In that case, make some decisions and move on. On the other hand, do not rush through this assessment. Finally, please be honest. You are not making any judgments about the parish. You are attempting to get a clear, accurate reading as to who you are and what the parish is currently doing in its social ministry work—something that is critical for success. It serves no one to be anything less than totally honest!)

SESSION OBJECTIVES:

1. To complete the parish analysis.
2. To complete a parish social ministry assessment.

OPENING
(15 MINUTES, INCLUDING PRAYER):

1. Call meeting to order.
2. Opening prayer.
3. Present session objectives.

PARISH ANALYSIS
(TIME ALLOTMENT WILL VARY. 45 MINUTES COULD DO IT, THOUGH):

1. Have each subgroup report their results from the parish analysis worksheets, guided by these questions:
▸ What did you learn?
▸ How/where did you get the information?
▸ Any problems
▸ Each group gets up to (but not more than) ten minutes to report.
2. Compile the reports into a single parish assessment.

PARISH SOCIAL MINISTRY ASSESSMENT & ANALYSIS
(45 MINUTES OR MORE):

1. Follow the instructions given on p. 27, "Nine Key Elements of Success: Assessment and Planning Exercise."
2. Based on this analysis, decide on one to three projects or ministry areas the team will organize over the next year. Make sure that you are attempting to move toward the full mission. That means that you will want to try to get beyond what you may already be doing.

These next few sentences are critical—please remember where we started this exercise. The role of this team is to organize teams of parish folks who, in turn, will be doing

Taken from *Parish Social Ministry: Strategies for Success* by Tom Ulrich © 2001 by Ave Maria Press, Inc.
Used with permission. All rights reserved.

the specific ministry (Direct Service, Legislative Advocacy, Justice and Peace/Global Solidarity, and Community Organizing). It would be a big mistake for this modest team to turn into the "doers" of ministry. You must concentrate on calling (recruiting) the rest of the parish to be a part of parish-based social ministry. It is both their right and responsibility. Your team must facilitate that happening.

Your next step is to begin a recruitment and organizing process to act on and implement the planning you just completed. Please refer to the chapter titled "Recruiting Leaders" to help guide your effort. You will know you have succeeded when you have recruited and organized a team of parishioners who see it as their responsibility to act on the specific ministry area that surfaced in this parish social ministry analysis and planning.

3. Divide the tasks for recruiting team leaders to head up the new efforts and assign those tasks.

WRAP-UP
(10 MINUTES):

1. Restate the objectives and determine if they were met.

2. Set the date for the next meeting. A sufficient amount of time from this meeting should be given to those doing the recruiting and organizing to complete their tasks. I suggest about six weeks. The purpose of this next meeting is coordination and trouble-shooting. You will get updates, assess progress on the tasks, and offer assistance where needed.

3. Offer a closing prayer.

CATHOLIC
SOCIAL TEACHING

BACKGROUND

Since the time of the earliest Christians, concern for the poor and care for the outcast have been major themes of our tradition. Often these themes are forgotten or take second (and sometimes third) place to other concerns, but when doing the work of parish social ministry, it is always helpful to remember that we are not alone. The gospels and over one hundred years of official teaching back us up.

The following pages are offered to help back you up in your work. They present the major themes of Catholic social teaching, the major documents written during the modern era on this topic, and some highly useful quotations from these documents.

The seven themes can be used in prayer services or perhaps to set the groundwork for a seven-week group reflection on parish social ministry. This is a good way to begin your work in the parish, or to refresh an already-established team. Bring together those folks you identified as leaders (or the existing team), and offer them a seven-evening retreat of sorts. Tell them it will only take an hour each evening. Present these themes to them in a prayerful, reflective manner. Read passages from scripture or some of the quotations that follow to accompany the themes. Ask the participants to write in a journal, asking how they understand it, and how they see its presence in their lives, parish, and community. What are some action steps they would see as important, based on these themes? Gather these ideas together, take care of whatever business matters you may have, and then send them forth with a blessing to live the Christian call to justice and peace during the week. At the end of the seven weeks, evaluate where everyone stands, and then either return to the ongoing work of the team, or begin the process as described in chapter four.

The themes can also be used to open your already-scheduled parish social ministry team meetings. Prepare to cut short some of the business end of the meeting for those seven nights.

Remember that prayer and reflection are critical components of the work of parish social ministry. Without prayer and reflection, we are not participating in the full mission. We can succeed only when we base our work on prayer.

CATHOLIC
SOCIAL TEACHING

MAJOR THEMES

LIFE & DIGNITY
OF THE HUMAN PERSON

▸ The human person is central, the clearest reflection of God among us.

▸ Each person possesses a basic dignity that comes from God, not from any human quality or accomplishment.

▸ The test of every human institution or policy is whether it enhances or threatens human life and human dignity.

REFLECTION QUESTIONS

1. How do you see the dignity of the human person being threatened today?

2. How does your belief in human dignity affect the way that you interact with others in the world? How would a lack of belief in a person's dignity affect interaction?

CALL TO FAMILY,
COMMUNITY, & PARTICIPATION

▸ No community is more central than the family; it is the basic cell of society. It is where we learn and act on our values. What happens in the family is at the basis of a truly human life.

▸ We have the right and responsibility to participate in and contribute to the broader communities in society. The state and other institutions of political and economic life, with both their limitations and obligations, are instruments to protect the life, dignity, and rights of the human person. Catholic social teaching does offer clear guidance on the role of government. When basic human needs are not being met by private initiative, then people must work through their government, at appropriate levels, to meet those needs.

▸ A central test of political, legal, and economic institutions is what they do to people, what they do for people, and how people participate in them.

REFLECTION QUESTIONS

1. How can we, in our parish life, participate in and encourage the teaching of the social dimension of the gospel?

2. What are the needs and pressures on family life today? What are some ways that our parish can support families as they deal with the needs and pressures identified?

Taken from *Parish Social Ministry: Strategies for Success* by Tom Ulrich © 2001 by Ave Maria Press, Inc.
Used with permission. All rights reserved.

RIGHTS & RESPONSIBILITIES
OF THE HUMAN PERSON

▸ Flowing from our God-given dignity, each person has basic rights and responsibilities.

▸ These include: the rights to freedom of conscience and religious liberty, to raise a family, to immigrate, to live free from unfair discrimination, and to have a share of earthly goods sufficient for oneself and one's family. People have a fundamental right to life and those things that make life truly human: food, clothing, housing, health care, education, security, social services, and employment.

▸ Corresponding to these rights are duties and responsibilities—to one another, to our families, and to the larger society—to respect the rights of others and work for the common good.

REFLECTION QUESTIONS

1. Advocacy is an essential part of "Rights and Responsibilities." What is advocacy and why is it important?

2. How does advocacy relate to our call to protect human rights?

OPTION FOR THE
POOR & VULNERABLE

▸ Poor and vulnerable people have a special place in Catholic social teaching. A basic moral test of a society is how its most vulnerable members are faring.

▸ Our tradition calls us to put the needs of the poor and vulnerable first (Mt 25: 31-46).

▸ We must seek creative ways to expand the emphasis of our nation's founders on the individual rights and freedom by extending democratic ideals to economic life and thus ensure that the basic requirements for life with dignity are accessible to all.

REFLECTION QUESTIONS

1. Who are the "widows, orphans, and aliens" of today?

2. Why does the church call us to an "option for the poor"? Where in the New Testament does Jesus show us a model in living with an "option for the poor"?

THE DIGNITY OF WORK &
THE RIGHTS OF WORKERS

▸ Work is more than earning a living. It is an expression of our dignity and a form of continuing participation in God's creation.

▸ People have a right to decent and productive work, to decent and fair wages, to private property and economic initiative.

▸ Traditionally, workers have the strong support of the church in forming and joining unions and worker associations of their choosing in the exercise of their dignity and rights.

▸ In Catholic teaching, the economy exists to serve people, not the other way around.

REFLECTION QUESTIONS

1. How does the church's call to the dignity of work and the rights of workers challenge us in a world with a globalized economy?

2. How does the work that you do give you a sense of dignity and a sense that you are contributing to the common good of society?

SOLIDARITY

▸ We are one human family, whatever our national, racial, ethnic, economic, and ideological differences.

▸ We are our brothers' and sisters' keepers. In a limited world, our responsibilities to one another cross national and other boundaries.

▸ Solidarity is the contemporary expression of the traditional Catholic image of the Mystical Body. "Loving our neighbor" has global dimensions in an interdependent world.

REFLECTION QUESTIONS

1. What does it mean to work toward solidarity in our lives, our parish, our neighborhood?

2. How do you build solidarity?

CARE FOR GOD'S CREATION

▸ Called to be co-creators with God and to have "dominion" over the earth, we are called to be good stewards of what God has entrusted to us.

▸ It is a requirement of our faith that we protect creation and each other from the harm that we can bring.

▸ The environmental challenge has fundamental moral and ethical dimensions to it that we simply cannot ignore.

REFLECTION QUESTIONS

1. What does it mean to be "co-creators with God," to be good stewards of God's creation, especially when it comes to the environment?

2. By sharing in God's goodness, sharing in God's dominion, having been invited to dwell in community, humanity is inextricably connected to one another, the earth, and God. Give an example of how you see this interdependence in your daily life, or the life of your parish.

Reflection Questions contain excerpts from Salt and Light: A Leadership Training Manual *by Peggy Prevoznik-Heins, Diocese of Wilmington, DE, Catholic Charities. For more information on this Leadership Training Program, contact the Office of Parish Social Ministry, Catholic Charities, Diocese of Wilmington, at 302-655-9624.*

CATHOLIC SOCIAL TEACHING

MAJOR DOCUMENTS

1891	Pope Leo XIII	*Rerum Novarum* (On the Condition of Labor)
1931	Pope Pius XI	*Quadragesimo Anno* (After Forty Years)
1961	Pope John XXIII	*Mater et Magistra* (Christianity and Social Progress)
1961	Pope John XXIII	*Pacem in Terris* (Peace on Earth)
1965	Vatican Council II	*Gaudium et Spes* (Pastoral Constitution on the Church in the Modern World)
1967	Pope Paul VI	*Populorum Progresso* (On the Development of Peoples)
1971	Pope Paul VI	*Octogesima Adveniens* (A Call to Action)
1971	Synod of Bishops	*Justicia in Mundo* (Justice in the World)
1981	Pope John Paul II	*Laborem Exercens* (On Human Work)
1987	Pope John Paul II	*Solicitudo Rei Socialis* (On Social Concern)
1991	Pope John Paul II	*Centesimus Annus* (The Hundredth Year)
1995	Pope John Paul II	*Evangelium Vitae* (The Gospel of Life)
1998	Pope John Paul II	*Fides et Ratio* (Faith and Reason)

MAJOR U.S. BISHOPS' STATEMENTS

1979	*Brothers and Sisters to Us*
1980	*Capital Punishment*
1983	*The Challenge of Peace*
1986	*Economic Justice for All*
1993	*Communities of Salt and Light*
1993	*The Harvest of Justice Is Sown in Peace*
1996	*A Decade After Economic Justice for All*
1997	*Called to Global Solidarity: International Challenges for U.S. Parishes*
1998	*Sharing Catholic Social Teaching: Challenges and Directions*
1998	*Everyday Christianity: To Hunger and Thirst for Justice: A Pastoral Reflection on Lay Discipleship for Justice in a New Millennium*
1998	*Living the Gospel of Life: A Challenge to American Catholics*
1999	*Faithful Citizenship: Civic Responsibility for a New Millennium*
1999	*A Jubilee Call for Debt Forgiveness*
1999	*In All Things Charity: A Pastoral Challenge for the New Millennium*

Taken from *Parish Social Ministry: Strategies for Success* by Tom Ulrich © 2001 by Ave Maria Press, Inc.
Used with permission. All rights reserved.

CATHOLIC SOCIAL
TEACHING

QUOTATIONS

You see, we didn't just make this up. The documents of Vatican II, papal documents, and the work of the United States Catholic Bishops demonstrate that social justice and the work of parish social ministry is truly central to our faith.

This section provides quotations from some of the major church documents on the preferential option for the poor and the concepts of charity and justice. These quotations can be used in bulletin announcements, newsletters, prayer services, and letters asking for participation on the part of parishioners. They are often helpful when giving presentations, especially when the crowd might be a bit skeptical.

I have found that one of the strongest arguments for parish social ministry is found in the words of the tradition. When people see that it has never been seen as just the work of the people on the fringe—rather it is the work of all the baptized people of God—it helps to move the issue forward.

In teaching us charity, the Gospel instructs us in the preferential respect due to the poor and the special situation they have in society: the more fortunate should renounce some of their rights so as to place their goods more generously at the service of others.

A CALL TO ACTION, #23

"If someone who has the riches of this world sees his brother in need and closes his heart to him, how does the love of God abide in him?" (1 Jn 3:17). It is well known how strong were the words used by the Fathers of the Church to describe the proper attitude of persons who possess anything towards persons in need. To quote Saint Ambrose: "You are not making a gift of your possessions to the poor person. You are handing over to him what is his. For what has been given in common for the use of all, you have arrogated to yourself. The world is given to all, and not only to the rich."

ON THE DEVELOPMENT OF PEOPLES, #23

A consistent theme in Catholic social teaching is the option or love or preference for the poor. Today, this preference has to be expressed in worldwide dimensions, embracing the immense numbers of the hungry, the needy, the homeless, those without medical care, and those without hope.

ON SOCIAL CONCERN, #42

Therefore everyone has the right to possess a sufficient amount of the earth's goods for themselves and their family. This has been the opinion of the Fathers and Doctors of the church, who taught that people are bound to come to the aid of the poor and to do so not merely out of their superfluous goods. Persons in extreme necessity are entitled to take what they need from the riches of others.

Faced with a world today where so many people are suffering from want, the council asks individuals and governments to remember the saying of the Fathers: "Feed the people dying of hunger, because if you do not feed them you are killing them," and it urges them according to their ability to share and dispose of their goods to help others, above all by giving them aid which will enable them to help and develop themselves.

THE CHURCH IN THE MODERN WORLD, #69

Love for others, and especially for the poor, is made concrete by promoting justice.

THE HUNDREDTH YEAR, #58

As individuals and as a nation, therefore, we are called to make a fundamental "option for the poor." The obligation to evaluate social and economic activity from the viewpoint of the poor and the powerless arises from the radical command to love one's neighbor as one's self. Those who are marginalized and whose rights are denied have privileged claims if society is to provide justice for all. This obligation is deeply rooted in Christian belief.

ECONOMIC JUSTICE FOR ALL, #87

"The needs of the poor take priority over the desires of the rich; the rights of workers over the maximization of profits; the preservation of the environment over uncontrolled industrial expansion; the production to meet social needs over production for military purposes."

ECONOMIC JUSTICE FOR ALL, #94

The obligation to provide justice for all means that the poor have the single most urgent economic claim on the conscience of the nation.

ECONOMIC JUSTICE FOR ALL, #86

The primary purpose of this special commitment to the poor is to enable them to become active participants in the life of society. It is to enable all persons to share in and contribute to the common good. The "option for the poor," therefore, is not an adversarial slogan that pits one group or class against another. Rather it states that the deprivation and powerlessness of the poor wounds the whole community. The extent

of their suffering is a measure of how far we are from being a true community of persons. These wounds will be healed only by greater solidarity with the poor and among the poor themselves.

ECONOMIC JUSTICE FOR ALL, #88

The quality of the national discussion about our economic future will affect the poor most of all, in this country and throughout the world. The life and dignity of millions of men, women, and children hang in the balance. Decisions must be judged in light of what they do for the poor, what they do to the poor, and what they enable the poor to do for themselves. The fundamental moral criterion for all economic decisions, policies, and institutions is this: They must be at the service of all people, especially the poor.

ECONOMIC JUSTICE FOR ALL, #24

SAMPLE BULLETIN
ANNOUNCEMENTS

See if these samples give you the inspiration that you need to write great bulletin announcements. Bulletin announcements can never be used alone to be effective—they have to be used with other forms of recruitment—but announcements like these will truly attract attention.

"Any human society, if it is to be well-ordered and productive, must lay down as a foundation this principle, namely, that every human being is a person, that is, his nature is endowed with intelligence and free will. Indeed, precisely because he is a person he has rights and obligations flowing directly and simultaneously from his very nature" (*Pacem en Terris* #9).

A Mass and Healing Service will be celebrated for victims of violence on Wednesday, March 4, at 7 p.m. A reception will follow in the parish hall.

FOR MORE INFORMATION CALL:

"Catholic teaching calls us to serve those in need and to change the structures that deny people their dignity and rights as children of God. Service and action, charity and justice are complementary components of parish social ministry. Neither alone is sufficient; both are essential signs of the gospel at work" (U.S. Catholic Bishops, *Communities of Salt and Light*).

The parish's St. Vincent de Paul Society is in need of 5 volunteers for its regular monthly visit to St. Bridget's Soup Kitchen. As part of the service experience, volunteers are asked to stay for the reflection and discussion with other members of the team.

FOR MORE INFORMATION OR SIGN UP CALL:

SAMPLE BULLETIN
ANNOUNCEMENTS

"The Word proclaimed in the Eucharist must affirm and celebrate the parish's work for charity, justice and peace. The Word must inspire social analysis and concerted action leading the people of God to a renewed commitment to the poor" (U.S. Catholic Bishops, *In All Things Charity*).

The collection for the Catholic Campaign for Human Development will be held in two weeks. Please join us in the Parish Hall after the 11 a.m. Mass next week to learn more about U.N.I.T.E.D., our locally funded Catholic Campaign for Human Development group. This is an opportunity to hear about a community organization in our neighborhood and to see the work your generous contribution supports. Coffee and donuts will be available.

"Christian faith requires conversion; it changes who we are, what we do, and how we think. The Gospel offers 'good news' and guidance not just for our spiritual lives but for all the commitments and duties that make up our lives. Living our faith in the ordinary tasks of everyday life is an essential part of what it means to be holy today" (U.S. Bishops, *Everyday Christianity: To Hunger and Thirst for Justice: A Pastoral Reflection on Lay Discipleship for Justice in a New Millennium*).

The Parish Social Ministry Committee along with the Liturgy Committee invites you to pick up the Advent Reflection Booklets to use at home with your family or small faith community. Each booklet includes the readings for the day, reflection questions, and journaling space for each day of Advent. They will be located in the church vestibule after each Mass beginning next week.

". . . [W]e are convinced that the local parish is the most important ecclesial setting for sharing and acting on our Catholic social heritage" (U.S. Catholic Bishops, *Communities of Salt and Light*).

Please join us for seven weeks of Catholic social teaching beginning Tuesday from 7 p.m.-8:30 p.m. Our speaker, Jane Smith from the Catholic Charities Parish Social Ministry Office, will guide us in exploring and reflecting on the Seven Principles of Catholic social teaching.

**FOR MORE INFORMATION
CALL:** _____

"In our service of charity we must be inspired and distinguished by a specific attitude: we must care for the other as a person for whom God has made us responsible" (Pope John Paul II, *The Gospel of Life*, *#87*).

Please visit the "Work of Human Hands" booth sponsored by Catholic Relief Services and SERRV International at the parish festival. Artwork and crafts made by people in the developing regions of the world will be available. "Work of Human Hands" supports low-income craftspeople and generates funds for the parish.

_____ **TO VOLUNTEER CALL:** _____

"We cannot be called truly 'Catholic' unless we hear and heed the Church's call to serve those in need and work for justice and peace" (U.S. Catholic Bishops, *Communities of Salt and Light*).

The Parish Social Ministry Committee invites you to attend our wine and cheese reception after the 5pm Mass on March 3. We will present Jane Smith with the Volunteer of the Year Award.

FOR MORE INFORMATION CALL:
_____

"The Church's teaching on international justice and peace is not simply a mandate for a few large agencies, but a challenge for every believer and every Catholic community of faith" (U.S. Catholic Bishops, *Called to Global Solidarity*).

Please join us in the school cafeteria next Friday evening from 7 p.m.–9:30 p.m. as we kick off our Lenten Journey. We will host a hunger banquet and hand out Catholic Relief Services' Operation Rice Bowl. Bring the kids and learn more about hunger and poverty in our community and around the world.

FOR MORE INFORMATION CALL:
_____

What follows is an example of a "quiz" that is a great discussion starter. I often hand out something like this when I start a talk, just to make the point about the depth (and sometimes the radical nature) of Catholic social tradition. You might be surprised at the response you get from such a quiz. I am giving you the answers separate from the quiz, so that you can photocopy the quiz if you like. I usually use it to break the ice a bit. Remember not to embarrass anyone who might have the wrong answer. The point is to show that all of us are in the dark to a certain extent. This is a discussion starter, not a discussion ender.

Answers:

1. A

2. C

3. B

4. C

5. A

6. A

7. B

8. B

9. A

10. B

A QUICK QUIZ
ON THE CHURCH'S SOCIAL TEACHING

(Identify the author/speaker responsible for each of the following quotations.)

1. *This, rather, is the fasting that I wish: releasing those bound unjustly, untying the thongs of the yoke; setting free the oppressed, breaking every yoke; sharing your bread with the hungry, sheltering the oppressed and the homeless; clothing the naked when you see them, and not turning your back on your own.*

    A) Isaiah (Old Testament prophet)

    B) St. John the Baptist

    C) Martin Luther King, Jr. (civil rights activist)

2. *You are not making a gift of what is yours to the poor, but you are handing over to them what is theirs. For what has been given in common for the use of everyone, you have arrogated [taken for] yourself. The earth belongs to everyone, and not only to the rich.*

    A) Karl Marx

    B) Plato (ancient philosopher)

    C) St. Ambrose (early Christian saint)

3. *The needs of the poor take priority over the desires of the rich; the rights of workers over the maximization of profits; the preservation of the environment over uncontrolled industrial expansion; production to meet social needs over production for military purposes.*

    A) Fr. Daniel Berrigan (Catholic social activist and anti-nuclear protester)

    B) Pope John Paul II

    C) Lech Walesa (Polish labor leader active in the Solidarity movement)

4. *At a time of rampant individualism, we stand for family and community. At a time of intense consumerism, we insist it is not what we have, but how we treat one another that counts. In an age that does not value permanence or hard work in relationships, we believe marriage is forever and children are a blessing, not a burden. At a time of growing isolation, we remind our nation of its responsibility to the broader world, to pursue peace, to welcome immigrants, to protect the lives of hurting children and refugees. At a time when the rich are getting richer and the poor are getting poorer, we insist the moral test of our society is how we treat and care for the weakest among us.*

    A) Democratic Party Platform

    B) Republican Party Platform

    C) U.S. Catholic Bishops

Taken from *Parish Social Ministry: Strategies for Success* by Tom Ulrich © 2001 by Ave Maria Press, Inc.
Used with permission. All rights reserved.

5. *We cannot love God unless we love each other, and to love, we must know each other. We know Him in the breaking of the bread, and we are not alone any more. . . . We have all known the long loneliness, and we have learned that the only solution is love and that love comes with community.*

    A) Dorothy Day (founder of the Catholic Worker movement)

    B) Fr. John Powell (contemporary Catholic writer)

    C) Mother Teresa (founder of the Missionaries of Charity)

6. *The Spirit of the Lord is upon me because he has anointed me to bring glad tidings to the poor. He has sent me to proclaim liberty to captives and recovery of sight to the blind, to let the oppressed go free, and to proclaim a year acceptable to the Lord.*

    A) Jesus

    B) Rev. Martin Luther King, Jr.

    C) St. Paul

7. *At the end of life, we will not be judged by how many diplomas we have received, how much money we have made, how many great things we have done. We will be judged by: "I was hungry and you gave me to eat. I was naked and you clothed me, I was homeless and you took me in." Hungry not only for bread—but hungry for love. Naked not only for clothing—but naked of human dignity and respect. Homeless not only for want of a room of bricks—but homeless because of rejection. This is Christ in distressing disguise.*

    A) Rev. Billy Graham

    B) Mother Teresa

    C) Archbishop Oscar Romero (martyred in El Salvador, 1980)

8. *Action on behalf of justice and participation in the transformation of the world fully appear to us a constitutive dimension of the preaching of the Gospel, or in other words, of the Church's mission for the redemption of the human race and its liberation from every oppressive situation.*

    A) National Council of Catholic Women

    B) Synod of Catholic Bishops (1971)

    C) Council of Trent

9. *The bread, which you do not use, is the bread of the hungry. The garment hanging in your wardrobe is the garment of him who is naked. The shoes that you do not wear are the shoes of one who is barefoot. The money you keep locked away is the money of the poor. The acts of charity you do not perform are so many injustices you commit.*

    A) St. Basil the Great (early Christian saint)

    B) St. Francis of Assisi

    C) Cesar Chavez (farm worker, union organizer)

10. *But this (charity) is not enough. . . . You will want to seek out the structural reasons which foster or cause the different forms of poverty. . . . You must never be content to leave them (the poor) just the crumbs of the feast. You must take of your substance, and not just of your abundance in order to help them.*

    A) Mother Teresa

    B) John Paul II

    C) Jesus of Nazareth

Author: Mr. Todd Graff, Diocese of Winona, Office of Ministry Formation, P.O. Box 588, Winona, MN 55987-5532. Reprinted with permission.

PROPHETS OF A FUTURE
NOT OUR OWN

ARCHBISHOP OSCAR ARNULFO ROMERO
ASSASSINATED ON MARCH 24, 1980

It helps, now and then, to step back
and take the long view.
The kingdom is not only beyond our efforts,
it is beyond our vision.

We accomplish in our lifetime only a tiny fraction
of the magnificent enterprise that is God's work.
Nothing we do is complete, which is another way of saying
that the kingdom always lies beyond us.

No statement says all that could be said.
No prayer fully expresses our faith.
No confession brings perfection.
No pastoral visit brings wholeness.
No program accomplishes the church's mission.
No set of goals and objectives includes everything.

This is what we are about:
We plant seeds that one day will grow.
We water seeds already planted, knowing that they hold future promise.
We lay foundations that will need further development.
We provide yeast that produces effects beyond our capabilities.

We cannot do everything,
and there is a sense of liberation in realizing that.
This enables us to do something,
and to do it very well.
It may be incomplete, but it is a beginning, a step along the way,
an opportunity for God's grace to enter and do the rest.

We may never see the end results,
but that is the difference between the master builder and the worker.

We are workers, not master builders,
ministers, not messiahs.
We are prophets of a future not our own.
AMEN.

Taken from *Parish Social Ministry: Strategies for Success* by Tom Ulrich © 2001 by Ave Maria Press, Inc.

96

PRAYER FOR
PEACE & JUSTICE

God, source of all light,
we are surrounded by the darkness
of the injustices experienced by your people,
the poor who are hungry and who search for shelter,
the sick who seek relief,
and the downtrodden who seek help in their hopelessness.

Surround us and fill us with your Spirit who is Light.
Lead us in your way to be light to your people.
Help our parish to be salt for our community
as we share your love with those caught in the struggles of life.

We desire to be your presence to the least among us
and to know your presence in them as we work through you
to bring justice and peace to this world in desperate need.

We ask this through our Lord Jesus Christ, your son,
who lives and reigns with you and the Holy Spirit,
one God, for ever and ever.
AMEN.

UNITED STATES CATHOLIC CONFERENCE, DEPARTMENT OF SOCIAL DEVELOPMENT AND WORLD PEACE, *COMMUNITIES OF SALT AND LIGHT: PARISH RESOURCE MANUAL* (WASHINGTON, D.C.: UNITED STATES CATHOLIC CONFERENCE, 1994)

JUBILEE
PLEDGE

A CATHOLIC COMMITMENT
FOR THE NEW MILLENNIUM

As disciples of Jesus in the new millennium, I/we pledge to:

PRAY	regularly for greater justice and peace.
LEARN	more about Catholic social teaching and its call to protect human life, stand with the poor, and care for creation.
REACH	across boundaries of religion, race, ethnicity, gender, and disabling conditions.
LIVE	justly in family life, school, work, the marketplace, and the political arena.
SERVE	those who are poor and vulnerable, sharing more time and talent.
GIVE	more generously to those in need at home and abroad.
ADVOCATE	public policies that protect human life, promote human dignity, preserve God's creation, and build peace.
ENCOURAGE	others to work for greater charity, justice, and peace.

Signature

The Jubilee Pledge was prepared by the Subcommittee of the Third Millennium and other committees of the National Conference of Catholic Bishops/United States Catholic Conference.

To order this resource or to obtain a catalog of other USCC titles,
call toll-free 800-235-8722. Visit the bishops' Internet site at www.usccb.org.

PRAYER FOR
A NEW SOCIETY

All nourishing God, your children cry for help
against the violence of our world;
Where children starve for bread and feed on weapons;
Starve for vision and feed on drugs;
Starve for love and feed on videos;
Starve for peace and die murdered in our streets.

Creator God, timeless preserver of resources;
Forgive us for the gifts that we have wasted;
Renew for us what seems *beyond* redemption;
Call order and beauty to emerge again from chaos.
Convert our destructive power into creative service;
Help us to heal the woundedness of our world.

Liberating God, release us from the demons of violence.
Free us today from the disguised demon of deterrence
That puts guns by our pillows and missiles in our skies.

Free us from all demons that blind and blunt our spirits;
Cleanse us from all justifications for violence and war;
Open our narrowed hearts to the suffering and the poor.

Abiding God, loving renewer of the human spirit,
Unfold our violent fists into peaceful hands;
Stretch our sense of family to include our neighbors;
Stretch our sense of neighbor to include our enemies,
Until our response to you finally respects and embraces
All of your creation as precious sacraments of your presence.

Hear the prayer of all your starving children.
AMEN.

Reprinted with permission. Cards may be ordered from:

Pax Christi USA, 532 West 8th Street, Erie, PA 16582. 814-453-4955.
http://www.paxchristiusa.org.
Item No. 552-244. $10/100 + $1.75 shipping and handling.

CONTACT INFORMATION
FOR NATIONAL SOCIAL MINISTRY ORGANIZATIONS

Catholic Charities USA
Parish Social Ministry
1731 King Street
Suite 200
Alexandria, VA 22314
703-549-1390
Fax: 703-549-1656
www.catholiccharitiesusa.org

United States Conference
of Catholic Bishops
3211 Fourth Street, N.E.
Washington, DC 20017-1194
202-549-3000
www.usccb.org

Catholic Campaign for Human
Development
3211 Fourth Street, N.E.
Washington, DC 20017-1194
202-549-3000
Fax: 202-541-3329
www.usccb.org/cchd

Social Development & World Peace
3211 Fourth Street, N.E.
Washington, DC 20017-1194
202-549-3000
Fax: 202-541-3339
www.usccb.org/sdwp

Catholic Relief Services
209 West Fayette Street
Baltimore, MD 21201
410-625-2220
Fax: 410-234-3183
www.catholicrelief.org

The Roundtable: Association for
Diocesan Social Action Directors
18 Bleeker Street
New York, NY 10012-2404
212-431-7825
Fax: 212-274-9786
roundtable@nplc.org

Network: A Catholic Social
Justice Lobby
801 Pennsylvania Avenue, S.E.
Suite 460
Washington, DC 20003-2167
202-547-5556
Fax: 202-547-5510
network@networklobby.org
www.networklobby.org

Center of Concern
1225 Otis Street N.E.
Washington, DC 20017
202-635-2757
Fax: 202-832-9494
coc@coc.org
www.coc.org/coc/

Bread for the World
1100 Wayne Avenue
Suite 100
Silver Spring, MD 20910
301-608-2400
Fax: 301-608-2401
bread@igc.apc.org
www.bread.org

THE MISSION & PRACTICE OF MAJOR NATIONAL SOCIAL MINISTRY ORGANIZATIONS

(In other words, so what do they do? What can I get from them?)

CATHOLIC CHARITIES USA

The mission of Catholic Charities USA is to provide service to people in need, to advocate for justice in social structures, and to call the entire church and other people of good will to do the same.

Catholic Charities USA is a membership organization based in Alexandria, Virginia. By providing leadership, technical assistance, training, and other resources, the national office enables local agencies to better devote their own resources to serving their communities. Catholic Charities USA promotes innovative strategies that address human needs and social injustices. The national office also advocates for social policies that aim to reduce poverty, improve the lives of children and families, and strengthen communities.

PARISH SOCIAL MINISTRY SECTION, CATHOLIC CHARITIES USA

Mission: We believe parish social ministry to be an essential element of living out our faith in Jesus Christ and helping bring about the Reign of God.

Vision: The Parish Social Ministry Section of Catholic Charities USA is a national network for leaders who are catalysts in their parish communities to come together, support and challenge each other, and live out the social mission of the church.

The Parish Social Ministry Section of Catholic Charities USA nurtures, fosters, and supports Catholic parish leaders throughout the U.S. in their direct services, advocacy, community organizing, and justice education activities. It is composed of professional staff and volunteers and strives to assist members by promoting education about Catholic social teaching, sharing ideas and resources, and offering training in the skills and strategies of effective parish social ministry.

For more information or to become a member of the Parish Social Ministry Section, please contact the Director of Parish Social Ministry, Catholic Charities USA, 1731 King Street, Suite 200, Alexandria, VA 22314, 703-549-1390, Fax: 703-549-1656 or visit http://www.catholiccharitiesusa.org.

THE PARISH SOCIAL MINISTRY REGIONAL TRAINING PROJECT

In 1995 Catholic Charities USA launched the Parish Social Ministry Regional Training Project using a grant by the Raskob Foundation for Catholic Activities. The Regional

Training Project is a partnership between Catholic Charities USA and a regional cluster of dioceses. The original plans called for holding nine two-day training programs over a three-year period (see sample agendas, p. 109). Catholic Charities expected this training to reach a total of 450 participants. To date, there have been eighteen regional training sessions given and over 1500 persons participating.

In 1999, the Raskob Foundation for Catholic Activities renewed its grant to Catholic Charities USA to continue the Regional Training Project. The new grant included a Core Training to those dioceses that have been unable to take part in this training and introduced a Phase II of that Project.

The Core Training provides the scriptural and theological basis for social ministry, aspects of the church's social teaching, and provides for regional needs. Phase II enhances and deepens the experience of the core regional training by going beyond the "basic training." This training targets those dioceses that have taken part in the Phase I core training and want to deepen their understanding of the social mission of the church. Both the Core Training and Phase II are offered in Spanish.

For more information on the Parish Social Ministry Regional Training , please contact the Director of Parish Social Ministry, Catholic Charities USA, 1731 King Street, Suite 200, Alexandria, VA 22314, 703-549-1390, Fax: 703-549-1656 or visit http://www.catholiccharitiesusa.org.

JUSTFAITH:
A FORMATION PROGRAM FOR WOULD-BE PROPHETS

JustFaith is an extended (six- to nine-month) conversion-based justice education and formation program that provides the opportunity for parishioners to study and be formed by the justice tradition articulated by scripture, the church's historical witness, and Catholic social teaching.

The aim of JustFaith is to empower participants to develop a passion and thirst for justice and to express this passion in concrete acts of parish social ministry. JustFaith is a tool that has proven over and over again to be an effective strategy for training and forming parishioners to be agents of social transformation.

JustFaith meets weekly, employing books, videos, discussion, prayer, retreats, and hands-on experiences. The intent is to provide a tapestry of learning opportunities that emphasize and enliven the remarkable justice tradition of the church.

It is adaptable to local parish interests and staffing. The syllabus allows for changes in the study topics and program duration and accommodates differences in parish staff availability and facilitation skills. While designed originally for parish use, JustFaith can be adapted for use anywhere, including diocesan-sponsored programs, small faith communities, high school settings, and college campuses. JustFaith also allows for

integration of "Journey to Justice," a popular education program offered by Catholic Campaign for Human Development.

For more information on the JustFaith Program, please contact Jack Jezreel, Director, Office of JustFaith, 7406 Greenlawn Road, Louisville, KY 40222, 502-429-0865, Fax: 502-429-0866 or justfaith@email.msn.com or visit http://www.justfaith.org, or contact the Director of Parish Social Ministry, Catholic Charities USA, 1731 King Street, Suite 200, Alexandria, VA 22314, 703-549-1390, Fax: 703-549-1656 or visit http://www.catholiccharitiesusa.org.

CATHOLIC CAMPAIGN
FOR HUMAN DEVELOPMENT

The National Conference of Catholic Bishops established the Catholic Campaign for Human Development (CCHD)—the Catholic church's domestic anti-poverty program—in 1969 with two purposes. The first purpose was to raise funds to support "organized groups of white and minority poor to develop economic strength and political power." The second purpose was to "educate the People of God to a new knowledge of today's problems . . . that can lead to some new approaches that promote a greater sense of solidarity."

The CCHD philosophy emphasizes empowerment and participation for the poor. By helping the poor to participate in the decisions and actions that affect their lives, CCHD empowers them to move beyond poverty.

CCHD has funded more than 3,500 self-help projects developed by grassroots groups of poor persons. Each year CCHD distributes national grants to more than 250 projects based in local communities. In addition, hundreds of smaller projects are funded through the twenty-five percent share of the CCHD collection retained by dioceses. The projects' successes and the relationships developed have significantly changed the lives of the poor in our country.

CCHD'S EDUCATION FOR SOLIDARITY:
CATHOLIC SOCIAL TEACHING AND ECONOMIC LIFE

This is a process that integrates Catholic social teaching on economic life and current economic forces at work in society. It seeks to demystify the economy and its impact on society. This training is a partnership between CCHD and selected dioceses. CCHD will assist dioceses that wish to sponsor a one-day training and follow-up activities. The training includes the use of presentations, reflection processes, interactive activities, and dialogue with CCHD-funded groups. The follow-up activities will be formulated by the diocesan team in cooperation with the CCHD national office.

The one-day training has three components:
▸ Presentation on Catholic social teaching as it relates to economic justice,
▸ Interactive session led by an economic trainer,
▸ Breakout sessions connecting the first two components to the local situation.

For information on how to bring "Education for Solidarity: Catholic Social Teaching and Economic Life" to your diocese, contact Mary Wright at 202-541-3374 or Andy Slettebak at 202-541-3376, Catholic Campaign for Human Development, 3211 Fourth Street, N.E., Washington, DC 20017-1194, or visit http://www.usccb.org/cchd.

CCHD'S JOURNEY
TO JUSTICE PROCESS

Like any journey that we take in life, the process of getting to our destination is often more important than the destination itself. This is true of the Journey to Justice process, which was developed as a means to implement the full mandate of the Catholic Campaign for Human Development. The mandate of the Catholic Campaign for Human Development is to address the root causes of poverty in the United States through the promotion and support of community controlled, self-help and economic development projects and through the education of Catholics on principles of economic justice and the importance of building solidarity between those who are poor and those who are economically advantaged.

In its effort to impress the circumstances that create poverty upon those who are more economically advantaged, the Journey to Justice process is designed "to effect in them a conversion of heart, a growth in compassion and a sensitivity to the needs of their brothers [and sisters] in want." With these words, the Resolution on the Campaign for Human Development adopted by the National Conference of Catholic Bishops in November 1970 set the groundwork for building solidarity between those who are poor and those who are economically advantaged. It is a solidarity that at the end of the journey creates communities that truly reflect the biblical principles of jubilee justice.

The initial event of the Journey to Justice process is a weekend retreat that is designed for twenty to twenty-five participants. This retreat consists of eight sessions that build on each other and represent a key part of the total conversion process. During the retreat, participants are led through reflection on and discussion of the scriptural call to justice and Catholic social teaching, especially as they relate to the preferential option for and with the poor. A major and key portion of the second day of the retreat is devoted to a lengthy immersion experience with a CCHD funded group (or other empowered low-income group as defined by CCHD and Catholic Charities USA). Following the immersion experience, participants are introduced to the concept of social sin and its relation to personal sin. This is followed by a session on social analysis within the context of the pastoral circle. The participants are then called to imagine anew what can be done to address root causes of poverty in their community. The final session is a call to commit to taking the first step to make real their image of a just community by agreeing to attend a post-retreat meeting. This is often done within the context of a liturgy.

The long-term outcomes of the Journey to Justice process are a deepening of personal faith, conversion to the justice dimension of that faith, formation of small communities of faith, leadership development on a parish and diocesan level, relationships of mutuality with empowered low-income groups, and new efforts of social action.

For information on how to bring the Journey to Justice process to your diocese, contact the Education Specialist, Catholic Campaign for Human Development, 3211 Fourth Street, N.E., Washington, DC 20017-1194, 202-541-3374 or visit http://www.usccb.org/cchd.

DEPARTMENT OF
SOCIAL DEVELOPMENT & WORLD PEACE

The Department of Social Development and World Peace is the national public policy agency of the U.S. Catholic Bishops. The Department has two permanent offices: Domestic Social Development and International Justice and Peace. The Department's goals are to help the bishops:

▶ share the social teaching of the church.

▶ apply Catholic social teaching to major contemporary domestic and international issues that have significant moral and human dimensions.

▶ advocate effectively for the poor and vulnerable and for genuine justice and peace in the public policy arena.

▶ build the capacity of the church (national and diocesan) to act effectively in defense of human life, human dignity, human rights, and the pursuit of justice and peace.

Due to the many and various resources, publications, and training opportunities provided by the Department of Social Development and World Peace, we recommend signing up for their "Issue Mailing," which is a packet of materials mailed out every other month or so (copies of the documents can now be found on their web page). Those who wish to subscribe to the Issue Mailing, the cost is $40 per year, pre-payable to: Department of Social Development & World Peace 3211 Fourth St., NE, Washington, DC 20017. Also, please visit their web site to learn more at http://www.usccb.org/sdwp or contact the Department of Social Development & World Peace at 202-541-3000.

CATHOLIC RELIEF SERVICES

Catholic Relief Services was founded in 1943 by the Catholic Bishops of the United States to assist the poor and disadvantaged outside the country. The fundamental motivating force in all activities of CRS is the gospel of Jesus Christ as it pertains to the alleviation of human suffering, the development of people, and the fostering of charity and justice in the world. CRS provides direct aid to the poor, and involves people in their own development, helping them to realize their potential. And CRS educates the people of the United States to fulfill their moral responsibilities toward our brothers and sisters around the world by helping the poor, working to remove the causes of poverty, and promoting social justice.

CRS OPERATION RICE BOWL

For twenty-five years, Operation Rice Bowl has been bringing families, parishes, schools, and other faith communities together during Lent to pray, fast, learn, and give. Operation Rice Bowl challenges us to put our faith in action and walk in solidarity with our neighbors in need all around the world. Through daily reflection, prayer, and action, Operation Rice Bowl helps you connect with your global community.

CRS FOOD FAST

Food Fast is a twenty-four-hour experiential hunger awareness program designed for youth in grades eight to twelve. It challenges participants to help reduce world hunger and poverty through prayer, reflective activities, and action. Food Fast challenges youth to make an active commitment to join in solidarity with their brothers and sisters around the world who are hungry. Through stories, participants will learn about Catholic Relief Services work around the world and will have the opportunity to pray for our brothers and sisters overseas who have experienced severe devastation.

CRS WORK OF HUMAN HANDS

This is an ecumenical partnership between Catholic Relief Services and SERRV International that offers hope and self-reliance by marketing handmade products crafted by low-income men and women around the world. Work of Human Hands helps:

▸ artisans receive a fair wage for their hard work through the promotion of more just trading relationships.

▸ grassroots organizations foster collaborative problem-solving and community development.

▸ our society counteract consumer practices that adversely affect the well-being of others.

Parishes and schools are invited to hold a Work of Human Hands sale. By doing this, you will help ensure that people all over the world have the productive resources to earn a decent living and be dignified members of the community. To order a FREE Work of Human Hands catalogue, please email: educationprograms@catholicrelief.org.

CRS GLOBAL SOLIDARITY PARTNERSHIP

Global Solidarity Partnership is a program that pairs U.S. dioceses with a CRS country program. It is designed to foster mutual relationships of solidarity through direct connections between dioceses and their parishes and the communities and local organizations where CRS works overseas. The partnerships provide opportunities for information sharing, education, project support, exchange visits, faith sharing, and

Taken from *Parish Social Ministry: Strategies for Success* by Tom Ulrich © 2001 by Ave Maria Press, Inc.
Used with permission. All rights reserved.

spiritual enrichment leading to greater action in the U.S. on behalf of the world's poor.

CRS HARVEST FOR HOPE

This is a particular type of Global Solidarity Partnership that pairs rural U.S. dioceses with a CRS country program that has strong agricultural programming. The shared bond between people who make their living off the land and the special characteristics of farmers and their surrounding communities are the foundation for developing a mutual relationship.

For more information on any of the programs offered by Catholic Relief Services, contact the Church Outreach Department, Catholic Relief Services, 209 West Fayette Street, Baltimore, MD 21201, 410-625-2220, Fax: 410-234-3183 or visit http://www.catholicrelief.org.

THE ROUNDTABLE

The ROUNDTABLE is the Association for Diocesan Social Action Directors. The ROUNDTABLE conducts an Annual Symposium and provides for exchange of information among its members through events, its newsletter, and through email and phone contact among its members. The ROUNDTABLE also undertakes projects such as the drafting of Standards and Expectations for Diocesan Social Action Directors, Choose Life! A Building Opposition to the Death Penalty, and Public Discipleship, its program for the development of lay leadership and spirituality for action in public life.

PUBLIC DISCIPLESHIP: LIVING THE FAITH

Public Discipleship is a comprehensive leadership development program designed to engage ordinary Catholics in the public dimensions of discipleship to Jesus Christ. Public Discipleship formation and training includes developing members' understanding of Catholic social teaching and its roots in sacred scripture, teaching the skills of public action and habits of social analysis, locating effective "vehicles for action," developing support through a small group experience, and grounding the entire experience in a spirituality of justice, personal prayer, and sacramental life. Individual membership in Public Discipleship involves attending two retreats, monthly small group meetings, and commitment to one or more social change "vehicles for action."

For more information on The ROUNDTABLE and its various programs, contact The ROUNDTABLE, 18 Bleeker Street, New York, NY 10012, 212-431-7825, FAX: 212-274-9786, or roundtable@nplc.org.

WEB SITES
AT YOUR FINGERTIPS

In addition to the National Catholic social ministry organizations, there are many organizations with a multitude of resources and activities for parishes to utilize in their social ministry efforts. Here is a brief listing of web sites that we encourage you to visit for more information:

Office for Social Justice – Archdiocese of St. Paul & Minneapolis
http://osjspm.org/

The Catholic Mobile - Theology Library
http://www.mcgill.pvt.k12.al.us/jerryd/cathmob.htm

Salt of the Earth
http://salt.claretianpubs.org/

Preaching the Just Word
http://www.georgetown.edu/centers/woodstock/pjw.htm

Jubilee 2000/USA - Jubilee USA Network
http://www.j2000usa.org

The Society of St. Vincent de Paul in the United States
http://www.svdpuscouncil.org

Center of Concern
http://www.coc.org

National Catholic Rural Life Conference
http://www.ncrlc.com

Pax Christi USA
http://www.paxchristiusa.org

Network: A National Catholic Social Justice Lobby
http://www.networklobby.org

Bread for the World
http://www.bread.org

Taken from *Parish Social Ministry: Strategies for Success* by Tom Ulrich © 2001 by Ave Maria Press, Inc.
108

SAMPLE
TRAININGS

The following are sample agendas from the Catholic Charities USA Regional Training Project. I offer them to you as an idea of what can be done in collaboration with diocesan offices. The trainings are organized at the diocesan level (in fact, several dioceses join forces on each), but the goal of the trainings is to enliven and support parishes in their social ministry efforts. Take a look at the topics covered, the prayer element, and the community-building efforts contained in these trainings. They have been highly successful tools, and I encourage each parish that is working on establishing or enlivening their social ministry to attend trainings like these. As I said in the Introduction, this book cannot take the place of an experience like a training.

PARISH SOCIAL MINISTRY
REGIONAL TRAINING PROJECT

Catholic Charities USA

Dioceses of Minnesota, November 12-14, 1999

DAILY SCHEDULE

FRIDAY

5:30 p.m.	Arrival and Registration
6:15 p.m.	Dinner
7:00 p.m.	Introductions
7:15 p.m.	Opening Prayer with Bishop John F. Kinney
7:45 p.m.	Theological and Spiritual Foundations of Parish Social Ministry *with Jack Jezreel*
9:15 p.m.	Social *hosted by Diocese of Crookston, MN*

SATURDAY

7:30 a.m.	Breakfast
8:45 a.m.	Morning Prayer (Winona)
9:15 a.m.	Realities of Poverty with Catholic Charities *with Greg Riegstad*
12:00 p.m.	Lunch
1:30 p.m.	Catholic Social Teaching: What & Why *with Joan Rosenhauer*
3:00 p.m.	Rest and Reflection
5:30 p.m.	Dinner
7:00 p.m.	Liturgy *with Fr. Richard Leisen*
8:30 p.m.	Social *hosted by Catholic Charities, Diocese of St. Cloud*

Taken from *Parish Social Ministry: Strategies for Success* by Tom Ulrich © 2001 by Ave Maria Press, Inc.
Used with permission. All rights reserved.

SUNDAY

7:30 a.m.	Breakfast
8:45 a.m.	Morning Prayer (Crookston)
9:05 a.m.	"Where Do We Go From Here?" *with Tom Ulrich*
11:00 a.m.	Evaluation
11:15 a.m.	Closing Prayer (St. Cloud)

PARISH SOCIAL MINISTRY
REGIONAL TRAINING PROJECT

Catholic Charities USA

Louisiana Regional Training

Acadian Baptist Center   Richard, LA

March 6-8, 1998

FRIDAY - UNA HARGRAVE, LAFAYETTE

4:00 p.m.	Registration begins
5:00 p.m.	Gathering Prayer - *Houma - Thibodaux*
	Welcome and Introduction - *Una Hargrave, Lafayette*
	Training overview - *Mimi McKelly Hartung, Parish Social Ministry Training Assistant, Catholic Charities USA*
6:00 p.m.	Dinner
7:00 p.m.	Session 1, Part 1:
	"The Theological Foundations of Parish Social Ministry"
	Polly Duncan Collum, M.Div., Parish Animator for the Glenmary Missionaries, former Director of Parish Social Ministry, Catholic Charities USA
8:30 p.m.	Vesper Service
	Informal Social/Refreshments

SATURDAY - MIMI MCKELLY HARTUNG

8:00 a.m.	Breakfast
9:00 a.m.	Prayer - *Lake Charles*
9:20 a.m.	Session 1, Part 2:
	"The Theological Foundations of Parish Social Ministry"
	Polly Duncan Collum, M. Div., Parish Animator for the Glenmary Missionaries, former Director of Parish Social Ministry, Catholic Charities USA

10:30 a.m.	Break
10:45 a.m.	Session II:
	"Developing Parish Leaders"
	Susan Stolfa, Consultant
12:00 p.m.	Lunch
1:00 p.m.	Session II, continued
2:15 p.m.	Reflection and Relaxation
4:00 p.m.	Session III:
	"Models for Responding to Multiple Needs in the Parish"
	Becky Reiners-Savoie, Parish Social Ministry Consultant
5:30 p.m.	Dinner
7:00 p.m.	Gallery Walk and Discussion Tables
	Becky Reiners-Savoie, facilitator
8:00 p.m.	Vesper Service - *Baton Rouge*
8:30 p.m.	Social/Entertainment- *Lafayette*
	Refreshments

SUNDAY - SR. MIRIAM MITCHELL, SHSP

7:30 a.m.	Breakfast
8:30 a.m.	Prayer - *Baton Rouge*
8:45 a.m.	Session IV:
	"Integrating our 'Mission for Justice' Throughout the Parish"
	Susan Stolfa, Parishioners from two "model" parishes share their stories:
	a. Lena Charles, Holy Ghost Parish Diocese of Lafayette
	b. Julie Delaune, Sacred Heart Parish, Diocese of Houma-Thibodaux
10:00 a.m.	Evaluation - *Mimi McKelly Hartung*
10:30 a.m.	Liturgy - *Fr. Ken Buddendraff, S.J. presider - New Orleans*
12:00 p.m.	Adjourn

PARISH SOCIAL MINISTRY
REGIONAL TRAINING PROJECT

Catholic Charities USA
Calling Our Parishes to Be Salt and Light
November 13-15, 1998
Holy Cross Abbey   Canon City, Colorado

FRIDAY

5:00 p.m.	Registration
6:30 p.m.	Dinner
7:15 p.m.	Gathering and Opening Prayer
7:30 p.m.	Theological and Spiritual Foundations of Parish Social Ministry *with Jack Jezreel*

SATURDAY

7:00 a.m.	Breakfast
8:45 a.m.	Morning Prayer
9:00 a.m.	Theological and Spiritual Foundations of Parish Social Ministry (Part II) *with Jack Jezreel*
10:30 a.m.	Break
10:45 a.m.	Expanding the Parish Ministry Vision to Include All Elements *with Susan Stolfa*
12:15 p.m.	Lunch
	Break
2:15 p.m.	Naming the Gifts We Bring and Calling Forth the Gifts of Others *with Susan Stolfa*
3:45 p.m.	Break
4:00 p.m.	The Parish Dream Team *with Tom Ulrich*
6:00 p.m.	Dinner
7:30 p.m.	Evening Prayer
8:00 p.m.	Happy Hour & Parish Showcase

SUNDAY

7:00 a.m.	Breakfast
8:30 a.m.	Morning Prayer
8:45 a.m.	"Where do we go from here?" *with Tom Ulrich*
11:00 a.m.	Evaluation
11:15 a.m.	Closing Liturgy: Fr. Don Dunn
12:15 p.m.	Lunch (optional)

SOCIAL DEVELOPMENT &
WORLD PEACE TRAININGS

The following list describes trainings offered at the diocesan level by the Department of Social Development and World Peace of the United States Conference of Catholic Bishops. These trainings can only be organized by diocesan personnel, so if something looks promising here, contact your diocesan Social Action office or Catholic Charities Office of Parish Social Ministry.

REGIONAL SOCIAL MINISTRY
TRAINING SESSIONS

These sessions, always planned in cooperation with other national Catholic organizations and local diocesan staff, are focused on building effective social justice ministry at the diocesan and parish level. They utilize the bishops' statements on *Communities of Salt and Light, Everyday Christianity, Called to Global Solidarity*, and *Sharing Catholic Social Teaching*. Ideally these trainings include two or more dioceses, they extend through a weekend, and they involve fifty to one hundred participants.

DIOCESAN PARISH
LEADERSHIP DEVELOPMENT

Diocesan social ministry offices often plan leadership training days for parish leaders. The Department of Social Development and World Peace offers speakers or specific sessions on sharing Catholic social teaching, the developing effective parish social concerns and social ministry efforts, building parish and diocesan legislative networks, and building a constituency for justice.

ENVIRONMENTAL JUSTICE
LEADERSHIP TRAINING

The Department of Social Development and World Peace's Environmental Justice Project has a variety of training opportunities available. Regional or diocesan sessions focus on building the capacity of the church to address environmental issues. Some funds are available to assist with these sessions.

SHARING CATHOLIC
SOCIAL TEACHING

Staff members of the Department of Social Development and World Peace are available to diocesan social justice and Catholic education offices to plan gatherings on how to more effectively share and integrate Catholic social teaching into diocesan and parish religious education efforts. Utilizing the bishops' reflections, *Sharing Catholic Social Teaching*, these sessions focus on the themes of the teaching and the concrete ways to more effectively share it.

DOMESTIC AND INTERNATIONAL
POLICY PRESENTATIONS

The Department of Social Development and World Peace staff members are knowledgeable on national and international issues of justice and peace. They are available to speak or present at diocesan conferences focusing on priority issues of the bishops' conference. Issues include economic justice, welfare reform and food stamps, minimum wage, food and agriculture, third world debt, foreign aid, arms control, and land mines.

Please take advantage of the expertise of the Department of Social Development and World Peace, and contact your diocesan office in order to invite them to your diocese.

HOW TO TURN A LUKEWARM PARISH INTO A HOTBED OF SOCIAL JUSTICE

By Jack Jezreel

Are you looking for a parish social ministry shot in the arm? Read how Jack Jezreel turned his parish around. JustFaith has been implemented throughout the country with wonderful results. Your parish could be next.

In 1988, I decided to give parish work one more try. I reluctantly accepted a position as minister of social responsibility with Church of the Epiphany in Louisville, Kentucky, a position that focused on what today we call "parish social ministry."

I confess my motives were mixed. On the one hand, I had spent the past six years in Colorado with a faith community modeled after the Catholic Worker and was convinced of the primacy of justice work in the life of faith. On the other hand, my previous experience with parish work and parish social action had been very discouraging, so discouraging, in fact, that I had decided to abandon parish ministry for farming.

But the financial reality was that I needed money to buy a farm, and so I consented with fear and trembling to try parish ministry again, at least long enough for a down payment on ten acres. I admit that I was at least intrigued by the idea that a parish would hire somebody full-time to do exclusively parish social ministry.

"I realize," I had written sincerely in my application, "that peace-and-justice work will always be done by only a handful of parishioners, that it will most likely remain on the periphery of parish life, and that it will be eyed suspiciously by most parishioners." One of the great graces of my life has been that I was wrong.

But it didn't seem that way at first. At my first monthly Social Action Committee meeting, four people showed up. At my second Social Action Committee meeting, three people showed up.

"This is not going well," I thought to myself. What to do? I had three choices, it seemed. I could take early retirement and borrow money from my dad for a farm. I could hope a lot of social-action-type Catholics would join the parish soon. Or I could try to figure out how to build a parish social ministry, something that I had never seen done.

THREE HINTS

The problem which confronted me was: how does it happen that any one of us ever moves from a life of disinterest in matters of human need to become absorbed in the life of compassion? The problem, I have come to conclude, has much bigger ramifications than I understood then, as I will explain later. But there were some hints.

The first hint was my experience in the parish. Despite my early frustration with parish life, I did have a very favorable impression of the Rite of Christian Initiation of Adults. I had facilitated the RCIA for various parishes for five years, and I was always impressed by the fact of transformation. As a matter of fact, it had been my only experience of seeing people change in the parish setting.

People who, for various reasons—some not altogether inspiring—had chosen to become Catholic often

experienced significant transformation during the time they were in the RCIA. Of course, this has been many people's experience with the RCIA around the world.

The second hint was my experience in the Bijou Street Community in Colorado Springs, an intentional Christian community modeled after the Catholic Worker. I was always curious about the fact that so many in that community had studied theology on the graduate school level.

This was not unlike the larger experience of the Catholic tradition. The movers and shakers in peacemaking and seeking justice have been people—often religious and ordained—who have had some access to more of the tradition than what most Catholics experienced in the parish. They knew who Saint Benedict was, they knew something about Catholic social teaching, they knew about liberation theology, or they had studied the prophets.

The third hint was the personal testimony of the great saints. It is the testimony of the encounter with the suffering. It is the story of Archbishop Oscar Romero, it is the story of Saint Francis, it is the story of Jean Donovan, it is the story of Jean Vanier.

"Our theology," says Father Richard Rohr, O.F.M., "is that we discover God in the eyes of the poor. Period." In other words, we need another set of experiences to mold us. We need to place ourselves in the company of the suffering, the poor, the marginalized, so that we can learn who we are, who God is, and what's to be done.

JUSTFAITH TAKES OFF

So, with little to lose, in the fall of 1989 I offered a program that I called "JustFaith." I advertised it as an intensive study of the peace-and-justice traditions of the Catholic faith. For nine months, we would meet every week for two and a half hours. Participants would be required to do a lot of reading (two to four hours each week). I also planned two or three retreats, some workshops, and some kind of interaction with the poor and vulnerable.

A fellow staff member told me that I had just planned the most demanding parish program ever offered. Of course, I had no idea if anyone would be interested, and I did not know exactly what we would do, and I certainly didn't know what would come of it.

As it turned out, twelve people signed up that first year. And the experience was nothing short of extraordinary.

So what did we do? To put it very simply, we read some of the best books I could find, we watched some very compelling videos, we discussed the hardest issues we could think of, we marched in a downtown rally after the massacre of the Jesuits in El Salvador, we listened to guest speakers and missionaries, we experienced an "urban plunge," we prayed, we had retreats, we became close friends, and at the end, we were all different.

In some cases, we were very different. And the people who went through that first JustFaith are today some of the pillars of the parish and the greater Louisville faith-and-justice

Taken from *Parish Social Ministry: Strategies for Success* by Tom Ulrich © 2001 by Ave Maria Press, Inc.

community. This experience has been repeated for each of the six years that JustFaith has been offered.

CONVERSION STORIES

The stories of transformation are many and powerful. Some are even dramatic. At least three participants left high-paying jobs for other work that paid less because of social-ethical concerns.

Pat Bowles left an engineering job with a major corporation out of concern for the dehumanization he experienced in the workplace and an interest in nurturing young people; he now teaches high school.

Mike O'Brien was the chief financial officer for a major health-care provider; he grew weary of the overemphasis on profit and longed to do something that connected directly with his faith. Today he works in development for a residential facility for at-risk teenage boys.

Tom Wannemuehler worked as a counselor and still does, except that now he oversees the care of the boys at the same residential facility where O'Brien works.

All of them would say that their experiences in JustFaith were the reasons for, or at least played a major role in, their decision.

Spouses Mary and Gary Becker went through the program together. Mary went on to become the chairperson of Louisville's Council on Peacemaking, and she started Louisville's only Pax Christi group. She also began her own business in socially responsible investing. Gary got involved with Prisoner Visitation Service, visiting federal inmates in Lexington. He also regularly works at a homeless shelter. Together, they have visited El Salvador and Haiti, and they provided a sizable donation to start a micro-loan program in El Salvador.

David Horvath oversaw the beginning of a sister-parish relationship with a community in El Salvador, which has prompted over fifty parishioners to visit this Third World country. Sara Kamlay continues as contact person.

Martha Davis is now on the local board of Habitat for Humanity and served as chairperson of the parish social-concerns committee. Rosetta Fackler spent three months in El Salvador and worked to create local markets for Salvadoran crafts. Chris Bowles began a parish committee trying to address issues of racism.

Rosemary Smith, Mary Sue Barnett, Jackie Claes, and Keiron O'Connell began a women's concerns committee and orchestrated a women's homily series that provided an opportunity for women's voices to be heard from the pulpit. They were also responsible for a yearlong program on the role of women in the church, inviting such speakers as Mary Luke Tobin, Richard McBrien, Mary Jo Weaver, and Catherine Hilkert, not to mention some outstanding local speakers.

David Chervenak oversaw a yearlong discernment process on the matter of civil rights for homosexuals. Bob and Dotti Lockhart have made at least eight trips to El Salvador, one lasting six months. Mike O'Brien is involved with a grassroots inner-city organization funded by the Campaign for Human Development.

Other participants have gone on to be involved in parish social-action

Taken from *Parish Social Ministry: Strategies for Success* by Tom Ulrich © 2001 by Ave Maria Press, Inc.
Used with permission. All rights reserved.

committees, legislative networks, material-aid collections, etc. Many have simplified their lifestyles—everything from moving to less expensive homes to eating less meat to just buying less. And many have become very generous with their wealth.

SIDE EFFECTS

In addition to these transformations, there were three other results that I had not expected and did not intend, but they speak volumes.

The first was that the people who went through the JustFaith process together often became very close. The experience of watching each other struggle, grow, choose, and change made for some very strong bonds. The difficulty of the choices they were trying to make and the common concerns for the world's poor and wounded made for ready affection.

Indeed, the testimony of many of the participants is that, over time, many of the former relationships in their lives gradually faded in intensity as their lifestyles and commitments continued to be molded by the gospel values of inclusiveness, forgiveness, and compassion. Meanwhile, the relationships that shared these values grew and became more important. I suspect this might have been the experience of the early church.

The second unexpected result was that, as we turned our attention to the external order, to the world and its wounds, there was a resulting need and appetite to address and more fully explore our own personal inner lives.

Thomas Merton was right: a caring look outside of us is somehow connected to a caring look inside of us.

Prayer and action are intrinsically connected.

In fact, for some participants, personal issues that had not been resolved even after years of counseling prior to JustFaith suddenly had a fresh and unexpected answer. I am reminded of one participant who spoke of her utter inability to heal a hate she had for her mother. It wasn't until she read Jim Douglass' remarkable book, *The Nonviolent Coming of God*, that she found some keys to reconciling herself with her mom. Personal and social redemption are so interconnected as to be indistinguishable.

The third unexpected result was the impact on the parish. By the third year of JustFaith, there was something of a "hundredth monkey syndrome." The simple fact of thirty-seven JustFaith graduates, energized and eager to be about social ministry, had an impact not only on spouses and friends but on the larger community as well. It surely wasn't the case that the entire parish embraced with passion the message and call of justice and peacemaking, but it was the case that the parish's agenda included more focus on such matters.

Thirty-seven parishioners working on anything might well be called a mass movement. That various matters were being brought before the parish council—such as requests to start sister-parish relationships with churches in El Salvador and the West End of Louisville, requests to fund new projects, and proposals to facilitate parish forums on environmental issues—meant that a great part of the parish's focus and agenda was being devoted to this business.

Taken from *Parish Social Ministry: Strategies for Success* by Tom Ulrich © 2001 by Ave Maria Press, Inc.
Used with permission. All rights reserved.

I believe the impact was, to borrow from the words of Peter Maurin, that it made it easier for the parish to do good. It also made, in my opinion, the parish a more vibrant, exciting place to be.

Now, after six years of offering JustFaith to seventy-five people, the work of social ministry is larger than one person could hope to manage. One hundred and twenty households are integrally involved in social ministry, with another one hundred to one hundred fifty supportive of various parts of the work. And, of course, each year another ten to fifteen people are integrated into the work.

The single most exciting dimension of all this is that now most of the initiatives and work of outreach, advocacy, and solidarity are authored by parishioners.

It would seem JustFaith has provided some critical insights that encourage the growth toward pastoral authority and action. But it may very well be that it is nothing more than the claim that deeply felt compassion—could this be what we call the "Spirit"?—has on our lives.

In any event, the work and projects grow. The maturity and spiritual wisdom increase. And some of the wounds of the world are healed.

NEW LIFE

The experience of JustFaith and its impact on Epiphany over the past eight years has taught me what faith, conversion, parish, and social ministry are about.

I believe conversion is primarily about the broadening and deepening of love—love for God, ourselves, for our neighbors. Any change— intellectual, practical, or spiritual— that allows for the expanded inclusion of the stranger, the enemy, and the suffering into the sphere of my care is holy.

Parish social ministry is simply the effort to organize the church's ever-broadening love for the world. The so-called preferential option for the poor, for example, is nothing but the church responding to the children of God the way a mother would respond to her own children, attending with special care to the needs of the one in pain.

And parish social ministry is at the heart of the Good News. It is good news, not just for those victims whose wounded lives might be healed by the work of compassion, justice, and peacemaking, but for the workers as well. It gives life and restores us as we recognize our common brokenness. And the paradox of the cross is something I have witnessed over and over again these past few years: the embrace of human suffering is somehow the route to resurrection.

I can only say that as people have healthily integrated social ministry into their lives, they have become more alive. They experience their own lives with more vitality. They are less attached to things that do not matter. They love better. They are more patient, more empathetic, more forgiving, more generous, more inclusive. What better definition can we give to "new life"?

All of this has caught me by surprise. I had not anticipated eight years ago anything like what has happened at Epiphany. And while I am sure such stories are told in other

Taken from *Parish Social Ministry: Strategies for Success* by Tom Ulrich © 2001 by Ave Maria Press, Inc.

places, I have been humbled and personally renewed by the lived experience of seeing so many conversions, so many deeds of courage, so many acts of sacrifice and care, so many caught up in God's mercy and justice.

I admit that I had at one time dismissed the parish as an ineffective tool for social transformation. I now consider its possibilities to be the most potent that I know.

And that is why, even after I bought my farm, I continue to work in the parish.

Reprinted with permission, *Salt of the Earth* Magazine, published by Claretian Missionaries. For more information please visit http://www.salt.claretianpubs.org or call 800-328-6515.

SOME GREAT BOOKS
AND RESOURCES

▶ *Catholic Social Teaching: Our Best Kept Secret* by Peter Henriot et al. (Orbis Books, 800-258-5838)

▶ *Dead Man Walking* by Sister Helen Prejean, C.S.J. (Random House, 800-726-0600)

▶ *Doing Faithjustice: An Introduction to Catholic Social Thought* by Fred Kammer, S.J. (Paulist Press, 800-218-1903)

▶ *Economic Justice for All: Pastoral Letter on Catholic Social Teaching and the U.S. Economy* by the U.S. bishops. (Call 800-235-8722)

▶ *Following Christ in a Consumer Society* by John Kavanaugh, S.J. (Orbis Books, 800-258-5838)

▶ *Gathering Prayers* by Debra Hintz. (Twenty-Third Publications, 800-321-0411)

▶ *Marketplace Prophets*, a video on economic justice produced by the U.S. Catholic Conference. (800-235-8722)

▶ *Parenting for Peace and Justice* by Jim and Kathy McGinnis. (Orbis Books, 800-258-5838)

▶ *The Prophetic Imagination* by Walter Brueggeman. (Augsburg Fortress, 800-328-4648)

▶ *Romero*, a film about the life, death, and legacy of Archbishop Oscar Romero. (Paulist Pictures)

▶ *Salted with Fire: Spirituality for the FaithJustice Journey* by Fred Kammer, S.J. (Paulist Press, 800-218-1903)

▶ *Social Analysis: Linking Faith and Justice* by Joe Holland and Peter Henriot, S.J. (Orbis Books, 800-258-5838)

▶ *Option for the Poor* by Donald Dorr (Orbis Books, 800-258-5838)

▶ *Preaching the Just Word* by Walter Burghardt, S.J. (Yale University Press, 800-987-7323)

▶ *Catholic Social Thought: The Documentary Heritage* David O'Brien & Thomas A. Shannon (Orbis Books, 800-258-5838)

▶ *The Fire of Peace: A Prayer Book* (Pax Christi USA, 814-453-4955)

▶ For a Free Publications Catalog of the United States Catholic Conference, call toll free 800-235-8722 or visit http://www.usccb.org.

▶ For a Catholic Campaign for Human Development Resource Catalog, call 800-235-8722 or visit http://www.usccb.org.